ASIA COLOR QUEST

-HALL

ASIA COLOR QUEST

Ronald E. Hall

To order additional copies of this book, contact:
Xlibris Corporation
1-888-7-XLIBRIS
www.Xlibris.com
Orders@Xlibris.com

CONTENTS

"All of us should embrace the vision of a colorblind society, but recognize the fact that we are not there yet and we cannot slam shut the doors of educational and economic opportunity"

President Bill Clinton, 1997

Dedicated

Dr. Gilmary Best, Dr. Creigs Beverly, Dr. Mamie
Darlington, Dr. Robert L. Green, Dr. Richard Lyle, Dr.
George Rowan, Dr. Victor Whiteman, Ms. Cortne Bui
and Chips

PREFACE

Although it is a less studied issue, the quest of Asian-Americans as pertains to skin color, and other post-colonial issues is no less significant. Considering scholars, there remain professors who are trained with hardly any reference at all to the implications of skin color in the aftermath of colonization. Local schools of thought dominated by the black/white dichotomy have failed accordingly to take notice of the growing Asian presence in American life. Furthermore, those who teach at some of our most prestigious universities, which serve a substantial minority population, have not the faintest idea of how the aftermath of colonization impacts social interactions.

As one who values knowledge, I have agonized over the manner in which people of color, including Asian-Americans, are regarded worldwide. On more than one occasion, I have encountered students, in social work and other human service professions, who are then trained to handle the keenest aspects of emotional and psychological adjustment with hardly any consideration given to the social and cultural gaps perpetuated by skin color. In fact, most social work faculties have gone through their entire educational experience without a word mentioned about color. It should therefore come as no surprise that students and faculties alike have not understood the role of skin color in the formulation of models and treatment strategies. For many reasons, the topic in practically every sector of the academy and the society at-large has remained an unspeakable taboo. I see this as threatening. It serves the tenets of racism and the post-colonial status quo. Subsequently, the Asian-American experience is then defined in context of the Euro-American social ethos.

The study of Asian-Americans in the post-colonial era can be neither understood nor assessed without a universal frame of reference. The chapters in this book will give readers some insight to the implications of skin color as pertains to Asian-Americans. It will characterize the taboo notion of hierarchy manifested on the basis of skin color. In this respect, *Asia Color Quest* is unique. It will take readers beyond the black/white racial dichotomy, exposing a demonstration of interaction among those who would be otherwise considered post-colonial victims. It will address the acting-out of post-colonialism as pertains to various Western ideals, including light skin. It is not an attempt to minimize white racism, or any other forms of Western social ills. It is not an attempt to criticize or pass judgment on Asian-Americans, but merely to serve as a mirror in which people of color may view a reflection of themselves. This should not imply my assumption that what is described is complete and accurate without flaw. Rather, it is an honest attempt to promote dialogue in the outcome for the book's ability to expose all forms and manner of colonial denigration. While I realize there are disadvantages in this approach, the most obvious of which is stereotyping and cultural misrepresentation by an outsider, I do not feel I have a choice. I am very aware and concerned about this and in no way wish to contribute to it, although I do not deny that what I have written can be misused by those who would choose to do so.

Some of my colleagues will argue that to write about the unspeakable will do more harm than good because it is so provocative. However, it is my opinion that confronting provocative issues literally is a healthy and socially appropriate way to benefit Asian-Americans and humanity in general; although said confrontation amounts to little more than a start, a start is where solutions begin.

In conclusion, I believe the problem for any writer who attempts to characterize a group of which he is not a member will always be that he may ultimately make errors of interpretation, which a native would not. When that interpretation reaches publication, we run the risk of doing disservice to all. In the grist of self worth, I have determined dignity and respect for people of color worldwide take precedent. The solution for me lay in maintaining openness and a willingness to confront new ideas. Furthermore, in the post-colonial era, those of us stained by the rumors of inferiority associated with our skin color indulge an extremely dangerous luxury. By virtue of our having been victimized, there is a tendency to portray us as simultaneously the embodiment of virtue and human piety. Our oppression by European colonials has cast upon our shoulders an ever-present cloak of white guilt, setting us morally apart from our oppressors. Some of us have come to feel that, because we are most often the victims of oppression, we have earned the right to cast a moral stone at our oppressors. We take no responsibility for social injustice whatsoever and have deluded ourselves into ignoring the implications of skin color because oppression via white racism seems worse. I am privy to Asian-Americans and other people of color who prefer the company of whites to their darker-skinned brethren in order to escape the painful color games. Such games have sent many of us to the madhouse. Thus, it is much better to expose the issue of skin color and other colonial dung than not, simply because it may be inaccurate or misinterpreted.

In the final analysis, humanity, of whatever gender, race or color, cannot deny the dignity and worth of another without diminishing some measure of its own. For in the image of one's victim is a reflection of one's self. Study the social quest of Asian-Americans to glimpse what we have become. Believing that, it is my sincerest hope that those who read this book move past stereotypes or misinterpretations. They should focus instead on the dynamics of our existence as closely linked members of a common genetic family.

Ronald E. Hall, Ph.D.

I

The Skin Color Issue

The genesis of skin color as a post-colonial issue among Asian-Americans begins with the origin of man and is purely a matter of conjecture. As recorded in numerous history texts, human origin relative to earth's existence began quite recently. The first appearance of homo-sapiens was, in fact, on the continent of Africa. Although the entirety of the continent is now inhabited, it is the southern region that is thought to be the birthplace of human-beings (1). According to Darwin, human-being as intelligent organism represents the final link in a succession of primates who would dominate earth. Whether one is inclined to accept this notion is arguably a matter of intellectual preference. However, few if any scholars will take exception to Africa as the location of human origin. Hence, every person alive today—including Asian-Americans, whatever their skin color, ethnicity, or native language—is at some point on the scale of human evolution the child of those descended from inhabitants of the "dark continent!"

Life in the south of Africa proved a perfect incubator in which the human organism could thrive and develop. The air was fresh and clean. The water was pure and plentiful. Abundant sources of game and plant life allowed for nourishment almost without effort. Additionally, the climate in southern Africa was so conducive to human existence that it was not an obstacle to be reckoned with in sustaining life. These nourishing factors no doubt impacted the psychological pre-dispositions of early mankind. Variations in skin color differed little if at all—that is, skin color was synonymous with today's relative dark (2). Thus, any distinguishable characteristics among the first human-beings were likely based upon some factor other than skin color, making skin color a less culpable issue.

As time passed, human life spread from Africa to other regions of the earth and differences in skin color evolved. Such differences would be exaggerated by Western civilization and defined by race. The idea put forth was that three racial groups of human-beings comprised a difference in kind and not variation. In fact, "race" refers to differential concentrations of gene frequencies responsible for physical traits which, so far as is known, are confined to manifestations such as skin color and/or hair form (3). Hence, there may be as much or as little physiological difference between the various race color groups as there is within them. While there exists no hard evidence that differences in skin color were brought about by regional location on earth, as conjecture it is no less valid compared to other theories. But if it is true that the original skin color of man was dark and that there is no genetic difference between the so-called races of man then any differences that do exist can logically be attributed to differences extended from regional location (4).

Variations in human skin color accommodated racial categories, which would dominate science as the crux of Western civilization (5). Scholars differ as to the number and nomenclature of race categories, but included in the discussion are Negroids, Caucasoids, and Mongoloids, i.e.: Asian-Americans. Every ethnic and national grouping of human-beings can be represented by one of these three categories. The first, or original man as far as archaeologists are able to determine, was a member of the Negroid grouping (6). Negroids are indigenous to Africa and characterized by dark skin, course hair texture, and broad noses. Caucasoids and Mongoloids by skin color and features are much in contrast to the Negroid. In Western nomenclature, Negroids and Mongoloids are referred to as "people of color," distinguishing them from Caucasoids.

In the post-colonial era, the ideology of Western civilization rests entirely upon the black/white dichotomy. Prior to the colonial era, color differentiations were first alluded to by ancient Greeks. The Greeks made reference to dark skin, however, classical authors had yet attached any basic significance to it. "Ethiopians do not astonish Greeks because of their blackness and their different appearance," wrote Agatharchides (7). It was apparent to him that such a fear ceases at childhood. Agatharchides' statement was not only an accurate assessment of the ancient Greek's reaction to dark skin, but it resonates today as an aspect of childhood not unknown to psychologists. "Four-year-olds," according to Allport, are in fact quite interested, curious, and appreciative of differences in racial groups (8). Furthermore, Marsh, in considering the awareness of racial differences in African children living in modern day Britain, found that the critical age of racial curiosity seems to be around three to three and a half years (9). Thus, it would be perfectly normal for a child living in a predominantly Western environment to take notice of darker-skinned Africans. The reaction of an African child, upon first exposure to lighter-skinned Westerners, would be similarly innocent and devoid of discrimination. In documenting his experience in African villages previously unexposed to Europeans, the explorer David Livingstone wrote that the moment a child came in contact with Europeans he would "take to his heels in a terror and that the mother, alarmed by the child's wild outcries, would rush out of the hut and dart back in again at the first glimpse of the same fearful apparition" (10).

The initial fear of children to peculiar skin color is normally short-lived, according to psychologists. That fear may not necessarily have an impact upon the later development of discrimination. In addition, there exists a strong indication that "whilst the development of race norms in children is logically contingent upon knowledge of racial differences, the obverse is not necessarily true" (11). Simply put, children may be aware of differences implied by skin color but will not necessarily attach judgments to them. This is especially true as pertains to the formation of stereotypes, unless they are exposed to socializing forces that emphasize overt racial identification and overt acts of racial hostility. To illustrate the point, Marsh proceeded to note that "such socialization forces were absent . . . overt race values, beyond those affective bonds formed in personal relationships, were also absent in children" (12). Thus, ancient Greek children lived similarly in an environment where dark-skinned persons frequented but where overt discrimination toward them was not a fact of life. Once they attained adulthood, such children had no reason to attach significance to differences in skin color or to think those of African descent were in any way fundamentally different and/or inferior.

Like Greeks, the non-"white" ancient Egyptians, whose contacts with dark-skinned people is seasoned, did not find it necessary to refer to Kushites—dark-skinned—by color. While Egyptian monarchs of the Twenty-fifth Dynasty, in their appreciation of art, painted dark skin when called for, neither the light skin color of the monarchs nor the dark skin of their subjects was seldom mentioned. The ancient Egyptians had for quite some time been completely at ease with the various gradations in skin color apparent among the residents of the Nile Valley and thus attached little if any significance to such differences.

In the dawn of Western civilization documentation of the attitudes toward dark skin suggests certain ideas were lacking. Greek references, however, are informative, particularly when they are scrutinized within the context of color. By virtue of historical record, it is possible to examine the early Greek norms for beauty and their implications for dark-skinned people. The combined Platonic, Lucreatian, and Ovidian assumptions of the classical norm image suggest distaste for extremes. The main characters in classical poetry seem to prefer their own skin color to that of the extremely light-skinned Germans and of the dark-skinned Africans (13). In the aftermath, like all people, in their expressions of aesthetic preference the Greeks used themselves as the ideal. Little mention is made, however, that there were Europeans as well as Africans who did not meet the Greek norm image. This omission allows for an emphasis upon dark skin that distorts the original view of Africans today.

In some early Western cultures there were those who extolled the beauty of dark skin and did not hesitate to do so publicly. Herodotus, the first known among Westerners to express an opinion about the physical appearance of Africans, described them as the "most handsome of all men" (14). Others put their feelings about dark skin into poetry. Such was true of Philodemus. In reference to a certain Philaenion, short, black, with hair more curled than parsley and skin tender than down, concludes: "May I love such a Philaenion, golden Cypris, until I find another more perfect" (15). Still, another named Asclepiades praises the beauty of the dark-skinned Didyme. The poem states: "Gazing at her beauty I melt like wax before the fire. And if she is black, what difference to me? So are coals when we light them, they shine like rose-buds" (16). Another named Theocritus contends that those who refer to his Bombyca as sunburned should know that to him she is "honey-brown and charming and adds that violets and hyacinths dark but are the first flowers chosen for nosegays" (17).

Citizens of Greek civilization maintained narcissistic norms for skin color. In referring to such norms for judging beauty, Harry Hoetink applied the terms "somatic norm image." He defines somatic norm image as "the complex of physical (somatic) characteristics which are accepted by a group as its ideal," pointing out that each group considers itself aesthetically superior to others (18). To illustrate the somatic norm image, Hoetink makes reference to an African creation myth. According to such a myth the African perceives himself as perfectly cooked while the European is underdone due to a defect in the Creator's oven. As a result, Europeans had to be fashioned from clay. The early Greeks would have noted that the norm for human skin color varied. The Greek Philostratus thus remarked that Indians esteemed "white" less than "black" because, he implied, "black" was the color of Indians (19). Among Native-Americans the creation myth lends further credibility to the innocent assumptions about dark skin.

As the Native-American story goes, the Creator was "baking" the first man. He fell asleep over the first batch causing them to burn—African. Out of anxiety, He removed the second batch too early—European. On the last try, the Creator made the perfect red brown batch who became Native-Americans (20). While containing a substantial degree of ethnocentrism, this Native folk tale is otherwise devoid of derogatory projections onto dark skin. While these Native-American creation myths are otherwise harmless, they are deeply embedded in the human psyche and are a prelude to skin color as a post-colonial Asian-American issue.

Skin color denigration and/or discrimination is not nor has it ever been the exclusive domain of the West. Throughout history many groups, especially those where the society was given to a military way of life, superiority was often motivation that prepared a warrior to win in battle. Although in its practiced form such superiority was in effect barbaric, the genesis of discrimination among others differed from that practiced in the West. African and Native-American cultures that appear to encourage it are more often an expression of exaggerated forms of ethnocentrism. According to Webster, ethnocentrism is an "habitual disposition to judge foreign people by the standards and practices of one's own culture or ethnic group"—much like the early Greeks. This does not necessarily imply hate, but appears to be more a question of familiarity. As a result, what emerges as different in this context tends to cease after a period of time under favorable circumstances.

The issue of skin color among post-colonial Europeans is unlikely the result of exaggerated ethnocentricity because the roots run much deeper and are more firmly entrenched in the Western psyche (21). "At least three quarters of the world population today is non-white" and/or dark-skinned (22). This fosters in "white" Westerners a psychological need for wholeness and belonging to the world community. Their immediate reaction is to denigrate themselves for the lack of something, which people of color have but who under colonization have come to denigrate as well. The psychological scenario is that Euro-Westerners desiring skin color, but being unable to achieve this end on their own, said in effect, consciously or unconsciously, that dark skin was disgusting to them. Subsequently, in the post-colonial era they began attributing negative qualities to color and especially to the state of darkest skin color. Anyone who questions this desire on the part of Westerners to have color in their skin need only take notice of the reaction to the first hint of warm weather as they shed their clothing and head for the nearest beach or tanning parlor. Most post-colonial Westerners cannot make the cognitive connection between this behavior and their feelings of color inadequacy. Thus only because the majority of the world's population contain melanin in their skin and the remaining one-quarter do not, Westerners have been predisposed to encourage the psychopathological affliction of skin color to another level (23).

The predisposition of Westerners to evaluate skin color in the post-colonial era does not appear quite the urgent matter that it is. In most instances, those who are afflicted display no psychotic episodes. They are well able to function within the context of society. In fact, some of the most respected leaders in American history, whom history portrays as otherwise, such as Abraham Lincoln, described themselves as being avowed racists (24). The fact that racial discrimination is acted upon with less social and political urgency has to do with its social and political dynamics. At its essence is the denigration of dark skin. No other element is as much a factor in determining how it is manifested and played out in the post-colonial social environment. Such an influence might be otherwise ignored and void of substantial impact were it not for the position of dark-skinned persons in relationship to the Western world power structure. Unfortunately in the post-colonial world, real power is synonymous with light skin, as personified in America's Antebellum South. Indeed, the greatest accomplishment of America's South is its success in suppressing guilt. Even in a situation where Southern slavery was profitable the likelihood of its wide acceptance in the face of guilt could not have prevailed. "Psychiatrists and other behavioral scientists frequently use the patterns of overt behavior towards others as an indication of what is felt fundamentally about the self" (25). Whatever the Euro-American concept of self, it necessitated that skin color play a major role in the outcome and extends to Asian-Americans and other post-colonial people of color.

By the time the post-colonial West had gained worldwide prominence the three racial groupings of man were euphemistically differentiated on the basis of their skin color, especially in the colonies. A Negroid was referred to as "black," the Caucasoid as "white," and the Mongoloid as "red," "brown," and/or "yellow," etc. The various designations of color do not necessarily pertain to the skin of each group literally, but instead serve as metaphor extended from race rhetoric. The issue of skin color has been dramatically played out in the all too often racist confrontation between dark- and light-skinned race groups (26). Much of that confrontation is spurred by the rhetoric of symbolism.

The consequences of Western symbolism exists as a by-product of projection. Projection was first alluded to by Sigmund Freud in his utilization of psychoanalysis. The objective of projection is the changing of the psychological situation by the subject to suit the subject. Projection is a critical component of the Western repertoire. It is used daily by Euro-Americans in reference to certain ideas and behaviors. If a particular behavior, in retrospect, appears to be "projection" to an outsider, it could never be recognized by the subject who would render it a completely different phenomenon.

Long before frequent contacts with Africans, the Oxford English Dictionary projected onto dark skin by assigning derogatory meaning to the term black. The more notable include, "Deeply stained with dirt; soiled, dirty, foul. . . . Having dark or deadly purposes, malignant; pertaining to or involving death, deadly; baneful, disastrous, sinister. . . . Foul, iniquitous, atrocious, horrible, wicked . . . indicating disgrace, censure, liability to punishment, etc." (27). Any form or human feeling associated with blackness suggested something bad or evil. That association even today connotes little difference between badness and its alliance with blackness.

Among a considerable segment of the American population exists a belief that the symbolism of blackness in Western culture has played a critical role in determining Euro-American perceptions of dark-skinned people (28). In the mind of the most typical citizen, the color black symbolizes lust, sin, evil, dirt, feces, death, etc. When Europeans first encountered Africans, they projected these derogatory connotations onto them, correlated in extent with the intensity of dark skin. Yet, in other Western civilizations including ancient Greece, blackness might find favor. Furthermore, certain scholars will note—for example—the positive regard for blackness in Western music. But the positive regard for black musicians hardly rescues blackness as a crux of Western disdain. It merely suggests an attitude less intense than either the "dominative" or "aversive" positions identified by Kovel (29).

Some of the common names for dark skin in the West are "sable", "dusky", and "ebony." Few if any scholars would suggest that such terms connote evil, feces, or death, etc., but it is only on the surface that such terms avoid negative connotations. If it is suggested that these terms negate assumptions of negativity by their relative sterility—what psychologists refer to as a reaction-formation against an underlying disgust—then in fact the argument for Western disgust vis-à-vis dark skin is made. Negative regard for blackness makes the point while positive regard proves the point since positive regards are clearly motivated by repressed feelings of negativity. Yet white is not necessarily positive. White, too, can symbolize death or evil in Western psychology just as easily as black, can as in sickness or as in Death's horse—traditionally pale (30). In brief, Western culture has traditionally accepted a "black" positive and negative as well as a "white" one. The symbolic meaning of "black vs. white" has thus never been simply equivalent to "bad vs. good." However, psychologically, blackness enables projection without limitation, as when Euro-American children/adults imagine things in the dark. This would suggest that blackness may be more potent than whiteness—i.e. light skin—could ever be. What's more, the act of projection will occur if and only if the projector has developed some need to engage in it. The question must then be answered as to why the need for projection—positive or negative—exists in Western civilization?

The implication of blackness in the West is not irrelevant to the treatment and perception of dark-skinned people. When dark-skinned men in particular were first encountered by Europeans in Africa, the reaction on the part of Europeans was one of immediate psychological shock. The intensification of fantasies around blackness was enabled by the fact that African cultures differed significantly from those in the West coupled with the lesser restriction of Africans to sexuality and their bodies. Aside from colonization, race and skin colors were initially less relevant. And at some point in time the Western regard for blackness, although intense, seemed to confirm little more than an extreme difference between peoples. But that difference was put to practical use by colonial Europeans who soon saw Africans as naked un-Christian heathens damned by birth.

The damnation assumed of Africans, and other people of color, was acted upon with intention by Christian missionaries. Ironically, their actions significantly enabled the denigration of dark skin. Enabling colonization, missionaries reinforced the perception of Africans as having evolved from the "noble savage" to the inferior savage, but savage nonetheless (31). This change was evident in missionary pictorial styles depicting dark-skinned people. Grotesque representation of Africans enabled Christian mythology by depicting them engaged in heathen rituals, idol worship, and cannibalism. Such depictions were significant in the Western characterization of the non-Western and/or third world. For centuries, according to African scholars, Christian missionaries rumored horror stories pertaining to African people without regard for their worth as human-beings.

To the credit of missionaries, denigration of Africa had begun long before their arrival on the "dark continent." Western writers

such as Cornelius Rudolf Vietor displayed shocking pictures of
Africa and Africans in their published works without having ever
visited an African country complete with biblical metaphor (32).
In the backdrop of this characterization the missionary was cast as
hero arriving in Africa to save Africans from themselves. This theme
became the plot of some of Europe's most popular and widely
published works.

Unfortunately, the attempt to Christianize Africans on the part of
missionaries was not very successful. This caused a hardening of view
toward Africans as heathen and uncivilized, contributing to their further degradation. The failure of missionaries to convert Africans was
attributed to the belief that dark-skinned people were devils in the
flesh. In 1854, one missionary wrote that the African heathen was
not only ignorant and weak, but: "the devil has exercised unlimited
dominion over them for so long that they have become his slaves and
have sunk into beastly and hellish conditions" (33). Such rationaliza-
tions of missionary failure became essential to the identity of missionary personnel. It also provided a means of differentiation between the
holy Christian brotherhood and their dark-skinned heathen subjects.
Regardless, the class status of the missionaries themselves was not
particularly as much of a contrast to Africans as they might choose to
believe. Not a few came from poor families and suspect backgrounds
that they were convinced were santitized in view of their whiteness
and Christian values.

In missionary imagery it is they—as white and/or light-skinned
people—who are both dominant and at the same time virtuous.
As pertains to Christian mythology missionaries are engaged in
work that is motivated by bettering the world and mankind in
toto. However, in missionary imagery the African is excluded unless denigrated or segregated (34). The usual roles played by Africans in their native culture do not exist. They were replaced by
images of light-skinned Europeans who all but edited truth and
reality. Thus, in photographs depicting African life Western priests
and nuns are seen as teachers, as caretakers of the sick and as leaders, usually accompanied by African children as opposed to adults.

Meanwhile, in Europe, missionaries enabled a Christian subculture conveyed by their actions, societies, letters, magazines, etc. Beginning in 1926, the Catholic Church sponsored an annual World Mission Day (35). The Mission Day vis-à-vis this subculture included Christian icons and statues of African children, suggesting gratitude for the missionary efforts. In the same time period Europeans could purchase African "heathen" children through "slave societies" (36). This was a Christian practice dating back to the Atlantic slave trade when missionaries could purchase children, rear them, and baptize them in mission homes.

The entire missionary apparatus represented wish fulfillment on the part of Western civilization. Meanwhile, in Europe, Catholicism and the Church were gradually dissipating. Thus in the course of the nineteenth century Catholic religion was relocated, abandoning the mainstream for leaving the periphery. While in Europe dissipation of Catholicism was on the rise, abroad Christianity was ascending. The rise of Evangelical/Protestant missionaries may have been the result of the Catholic church's loss of ground in the West. The Evangelical/Protestant missions did not get involved with Africans until after 1790 and in the early nineteenth century (37).

The position of the Catholic Church was that, aside from declines, the missionary culture needed rejuvenation. Catholic missionaries conveyed the impression of the Church as the answer at a time in Europe when the Church was being threatened by advances in secularism and socialism (38). While converted Africans in France sang "Save, save France in the name of the Sacred Heart," in Belgium missionaries held performances where they would dress up as Africans in black-face and straw skirts singing: "Have Pity, have pity, I have a soul like thee" (39).

It is debatable as to whether or not Christian missions accomplished their objectives. At least in terms of economics, returns on investments were quite modest. Among Africans and other people of color in the third world, Christianity was losing ground to the movement of Islam. Islam continued to spread without employing missionaries, money, or governmental support to Africa and parts of Asia. It benefited greatly in its appeal to people of color, not only by its professed egalitarianism but also by recognition of the assumed superiority of missionaries to their subjects. European colonization and conquest played a role as well.

The effectiveness of Christianity in Africa was primarily in conjunction with colonization. With religion at the forefront, the West gained access assisted by Africans in the many independent Churches that evolved. Ironically, it was the independent churches that spurred much of the nationalist resistance, in contrast to the traditional churches, which were little more than extensions of the colonial state. That state has maintained influence on how Africans are perceived in the West within a more post-colonial context.

Conspicuous by dark skin, Western explorers created an image of Africans as inhabitants of the forbidden "dark continent." At the zenith of its influence, Europe conveyed Africans as heathen and the ignoble savages to justify discrimination. Altogether demonization of Africa gave license to the West to exploit dark-skinned people in any way it saw fit. Furthermore, the post-colonial image of the West was served by denigrating nations inhabited by dark-skinned people. The various denominations of Western Christianity were invigorated by the glamour and prestige brought by the missions. Eventually the denigration of Africa enabled discrimination against dark-skinned people to become acceptable not only in Europe but the totality of the Western world, including people of color who made it their homeland.

Christian mythology contributed to the issue of skin color evident in the depiction of dark-skinned people. By cultural myth extended from biblical tales, dark-skinned Africans had been effectively demonized. The most noted of such tales is that of Ham. According to Christian tradition, Africans are descendants of Ham. Ham was the son of Noah. As the story goes, Ham was to have looked upon his father naked—a strong sexual implication. As punishment for this indiscretion, God was said to have willed that Ham's son and all his descendants would be black.

The association of Africans with Ham provided a convenient colonial mechanism for accusations of their rejecting paternal authority by Western commentators. The blackening and rejection of Ham's descendants then represents—according to Christian mythology—the retaliatory castration by the higher Father in God. As per Freud's psychoanalysis, what is black and/or banished would not be seen, as when King Oedipus was said to have blinded and banished himself for learning of what he had done. After punishing one among their number, Noah's remaining sons then earned the approval and protection of God, their paternal Father. This scenario rationalized colonial oppression in the West and cultural absorption of the superego. It furthermore contributed to the issue of color consciousness. The bad and evil son, set apart from humanity by the curse of dark skin, had been forever banished from the acceptable fold of humanity until the European descendants of the white sons of Noah discovered him again, presumably in Africa (40).

In more modern post-colonial times, Western scholars sought to scientifically rationalize the story of Ham. One of their first attempts to account for dark and/or black skin was to say it was due to the intense sun in the African region. This hypothesis did not last very long considering that there were Native-Americans on a similar latitude in the New World, who by comparison, were quite light-skinned. In the minds of the most learned among men, the myth of Ham was utilized to account for what could not be substantiated scientifically. Subsequently it became suitable for Europeans, enabled by psychodynamics, to inculcate the view that the bodies of the dark-skinned peoples of Africa were the manifestation of the most primal of curses among mankind. These assumptions formed the bases for the many fantasies surrounding race. However, such fantasies prior to European colonization had yet to be applied to an abstract concept of race per se, but they did encourage justification for slavery and notions of the "white man's burden." The eventuality of an Atlantic slave trade and Western colonization brought about fantasies pertaining to blackness, and

associated with dark-skinned people, which grew in intensity cul-
minating in racial mythology. Thus, among civilized nations in
Europe and elsewhere people of color—Africans in particular—
represented the embodiment of psychological filth and emotional
disgust.

Returning to Freud's concept of psychoanalysis, motivated by
the super-ego, the ego designated the id, something not seen, as
being associated with darkness i.e.: black. Thus, the id represents
blackness within the personality. Its underlying components, repressed from consciousness, reveal themselves symbolically vis-à-
vis fantasies of dark skin.

In Freud's psychodynamics of blackness, Western civilization
has revealed by way of projection how it has acted upon the revela-
tion of dark-skinned people. Christianity has assumed the task of
being a direct representative of the culture that destroyed African
civilization necessitating among Africans the need for missionary
assistance. That dual role makes it an appropriate sacrifice, in the
blackness myth, to the more barbaric entity that it serves. Thus,
having wedged itself securely into the Western psyche, dark skin
via blackness dominates as the focus of the skin color issue. Psychodynamically, Western culture has found a way to resolve—
through projection—much of its color conflict at the expense of
dark-skinned people. It was a convenient justification for slavery.
Vis-à-vis the myth of race, the "white" man was psychologically
free—that is without guilt—to exploit Africans and other people
of color. This ability allowed for the unconscious oedipal symbolism without inhibition to be acted out in real life. The Antebellum maternal figure is thus divided into the pure "white" mother
and the impure, lustful "black" "mammy." The "black" man represents divided roles of bad father to be castrated and bad son, Ham,
to be castrated as punishment for castrating his father—Noah. He
is also the end of projected oedipal desires for the Antebellum
"white" mother. The "black" woman becomes a sexually available
object for repressed "white" oedipal desires for the mother while at
the same time symbolizing lust.

The psychodynamic of Western projection is not without consequences to the "black" male and "white" psyche. The situation ultimately deprives "white" women of full maternal and sexual gratification. For "black" males there is self-hatred and passivity. The highly sexualized ritual of Southern slavery is obvious in its preoccupation with the "black" male rapist of "white" women, castration as a punishment during lynchings, and sexual exploitation of the "black" woman—not to mention exaggerated religiosity.

In the post-colonial aftermath of the Antebellum, a new form of skin color denigration has emerged in the figurement of aversion. The previously omnipotent Southern "white" slave-owner had created a situation where he could act out his oedipal fantasies and conflicts free of consequence. The dark-skinned descendants of slaves have now become the very symbol of these atrocities and something to be avoided in polite circles. Christian scholars continue to support that effort. Psychodynamically it follows that Southern—and Northern—segregation is regarded as a shift from an id-dominated slave culture to an ego-dominated one, giving way to a clean, rational, hard-working and self-controlled American citizen. Their penchant for projection victimizes dark-skinned people—African-Americans in particular—as adversary. They are presumed dirty, emotional, lazy, violent, and lacking in self-control, especially where sexuality is concerned. This more subtle form of skin color denigration is evident in the need for a Civil Rights struggle, Affirmative Action, and other post-colonial controversies. Passive-aggressive denigration has thus become the mainstay for denigrating people of color.

By psychoanalysis of post-colonial America the earliest distinctions between dirt and purity have been enabled by religion, Western symbolism, and projection (41). The aftermath of colonization had been reinforced by culture and the influence of aggressive Western groups. Such distinctions were carried to the extreme via the domination of people of color and projected onto them in a way that defied logic (42). The projections onto dark skin also enabled sexual overtones given the proximity of genitalia to excrement. This intensified a libido driven conflict reflected in the various forms of neurosis characteristic of Western sexuality (43). Ultimately the consequence of taboos have sustained a system of "white" (light-skinned) privilege in America and elsewhere, where skin color of the peoples vary from light to dark.

The senses of touch, smell, taste, and, most importantly, sight allow for the projection of abhorrence onto human groups. It culminates in the concept of dirt and other derogatory filth (44). Its dark color conveyed by the sense of sight allows for projections onto persons by virtue of their characterization as same. They are then cast as the physiological embodiment of psychic filth and inevitably devalued as human because they are dark (45).

In the works of Freud, there are few references to the social and psychological potency of skin color (46). During his era, dark-skinned subjects were discriminated against with minimal consequence. Freud's lack of attention to this psychoanalytically rich phenomenon may have been a reflection of dirt fantasies in which the personal tragedies of dark-skinned people were simply irrelevant to mainstream scholarship (47). Heretofore, skin color denigration has been less overt and more covert, lodged firmly in the Western subconscious. But the subconscious fantasies from which norms are fashioned may in affect be more potent than reality itself. Such fantasies are a form of purification reflected in Western culture's obsession with cleanliness. This obsession was likely unknown among primitives (48). Dirt in the form of excrement is externalized to the outside world and projected by norm onto dark-skinned people who must then thrive despite its implications. The objective of projection must be from the body to the outside world. If this is true, all things viewed as dirty or disgusting represent those aspects of the body and its waste products, hence the psychologically justifiable normalization of light skin by post-colonial American institutions (49).

Reinforced by religion, projection, and psycholanalysis the issue of skin color is also located in American history. As is well known, Columbus "discovered" America in 1492. Never mind that

Africans and other groups had touched the shores of this great nation long before the 15th century naval powers arrived (50). Such historical deception was a clue to many of the interpretations of history that would later come to pass. To begin, Native-Americans—Asian in appearance—are not "Indians." Indian is a name given them by Columbus having thought he had discovered a new route to India—another Asian group. Nevertheless, as people of color the American Indian, following the African, is the aboriginal inhabitant of the Americas.

Upon the arrival of Columbus, Indians roamed the open plains of America a proud free people of diverse cultures and colors. Since that time they have been subjected to some of the cruelest instances of racism, often in the name of religious conviction. As will be discussed later many such cruelties contained sexual overtones as well. "A particularly bloody incident occurred in 1864, when Colonel John Chivington, a Christian minister, led a band of Colorado volunteers who massacred nearly 200 peace-seeking Indians at Sand Creek. Both male and female genitals were later exhibited by victors as they marched into Denver" (51). When men go to war to defend themselves and family it is not difficult to rationalize in the context of mental health. That anyone could delight in war is without a doubt an instance of mental and emotional disturbance. As cruel an account of history this might be the discriminatory attitude that motivated it prevails.

In a similar post-colonial Western atrocity, South Africa is a land where millions of dark-skinned people have resided literally thousands of years. In fact, Europeans in this area are little more than foreigners. Their interaction with native Africans exemplify deep rooted fear. Either they dominate or assume people of color will take control (52). In the mind of the Afrikanner this is the cruelest of fates. To rationalize such fears, the black African in the mind of the Afrikanner has been debased and dehumanized. That South Africa has been freed offers little solace to its native African people. What happened to Indians and what is happening to South Africans is not uncommon. A similar scenario occurred in post-colonial Australia, New Zealand, South America, Canada, and various other places inhabited by people of color.

Characteristic of the post-colonial era, people of color exist in a world both dissimilar and yet oblivious to the dynamics of dissimilarity. It is crystal-clear, however, that skin color is without a doubt among the most critical of traits by which the races of Western society can be readily assessed. While the work of scholars tends to focus on the Americas, where the issue of skin color can be observed in some of its most violent forms, it must be recognized that, to one degree or another, skin color all but dictates the post-colonial social environment (53). Furthermore, since color implies the characteristics of a person, rather than the person himself, its existence as an issue accommodates an emotional reaction to an otherwise benign physiological trait. Variations in skin color couched in history, and given the esteem of Western civilization, may significantly impact the future quality of life on earth. That does not establish conclusively that skin color was among the earliest sensibilities of man. But the tenacity of this trait over post-colonial history is, however, an undeniable fact. Thus, human interaction has involved all too often the confrontation—both imagined and real—between people of varying skin colors. In the aftermath invariably are the humiliation, insult, and injury of one by the other.

Assuming that skin color constitute the basis or rationale for colonization, it will then constitute the rationale for differentiation and preference within a given Western society including its citizenry. Hence, in post colonial America people of the same or similar skin color frequently share common experiences, such as proximity to physical norms and/or superior socioeconomic status (54). For those whose color contrasts with the norm may be assignment to a degraded status, which serves to intensify the color affinity. Even where there had been minimal tendency in this direction, any segmentation has the effect of under-scoring what was, at the outset, trivial. Accordingly, it thus makes possible a universal hierarchy and tension between and within a given group(s) of people irrespective of race.

Although skin color denigration is not unique to Western culture, the Yankee version is distinguishable. Its impact upon various factions of the world population is tenacious and evident via daily racial contact. That contact determines the behavior of male as well as female, child as well as adult, and throughout the world victim as well as perpetrator. Even in the most intimate moments between two human beings an exchange may reveal some element motivated by skin color. It is from this most fundamental psychological level that denigration has evolved. For the individual, detection of it may be obvious. For the group of said individual, however, the phenomenon is a bit more complex. The elusive and more abstract dynamics of group interaction can only be discovered and/or substantiated by way of analysis designed to suit the task. Such task includes an analysis of the relationship between man and his environment, more specifically, how Western groups within the human species encouraged behaviors that were passed on to foreign and future generations and permeated the most primal corners of the human psyche (55).

Although the issue of skin color has not risen to the level of consciousness for many, it remains just below the surface. Such an issue is more often acted out in the aftermath of colonization of third world countries. Malcolm X was fond of making the remark, "When Columbus "discovered" America the Europeans had the bible and the Indians the land. By the time they left, the Indians had the bible and the Europeans the land" (56). Throughout history wherever Western aggression has been acted out it was rationalized in the context of rescuing the dark-skinned "heathens" from their barbarism. Eventual colonization then became a matter of mankind assisting itself in the evolution of civilization. The fact that the African and Indian's experience with Western colonization was rendered progress, post-colonial America is couched in greatness. However, there is probably some faction within any group, that is capable of acting out aggression absent guilt. But, the essence of this matter is the suppressing effect which it has had upon an otherwise well-adjusted and healthy national psyche. As long as this continues, guilt will never be an element in curing America of its color ailment. Its tenacity among people of color—including Asian-Americans—extends directly from that fact as prelude to various manifestations of racism.

References

(1) Rogers, J. (1967). Sex and Race. St. Petersburg, FL., Rogers.

(2) Ibid

(3) Ibid

(4) Bradley, M. (1978). The Ice man inheritance. Toronto, Dorset.

(5) Hirschman, C. & Kraly, E. (1990). Racial and ethnic inequality in the United States, 1940 and 1950: the impact of geographic location and human capital. International Migration Review, vol 24, 1, p. 4-33.

(6) Rogers, J. (1967). Sex and Race. St. Petersburg, FL., Rogers.

(7) Snowden, F. (1983). Before color prejudice. Cambridge, MA. Harvard University Press.

(8) Ibid

(9) Ibid

(10) Ibid

(11) Ibid

(12) Ibid

(13) Ibid

(14) Ibid

(15) Ibid

(16) Ibid

(17) Ibid

(18) Ibid

(19) Norton, D. (1993). Diversity, early socialization, and temporal development: The dual perspective revisited. Social Work. January, Vol 38(1), 82-90.

(20) Yellow Bird, M. (1995). Spirituality in first nations story telling: A Sahnish-hidasta approach to narrative. Reflections, 1(4), pp. 65-72.

(21) Kovel, J. (1984). White discrimination: A psychohistory. New York: Columbia University Press.

(22) Welsing, F. (1970). The Cress Theory of Color Confrontation and Discrimination. Washington, D.C.: C-R Publishers.

(23) Stember, C. (1976). Sexual Discrimination. New York: Elsevier Scientific.

(24) Kovel, J. (1984). White discrimination: A psychohistory. New York: Columbia University Press.

(25) Ibid

(26) Hall, R. E. (Winter, 1995/96). Dark skin and the cultural ideal of masculinity. Journal of African American Men. 1(3), 37-62.

(27) Richards, G. (1997). Race, Racism and Psychology. Rutledge, New York.

(28) Ibid

(29) Kovel, J. (1984). White discrimination: A psychohistory. New York: Columbia University Press.

(30) Pieterse, J. (1992). White on Black. Yale University Press, New Haven, CN.

(31) Ibid

(32) Ibid

(33) Ibid

(34) Ibid

(35) Ibid

(36) Ibid

(37) Ibid

(38) Ibid

(39) Ibid

(40) Richards, G. (1997). Race, Racism and Psychology. Rutledge, New York.

(41) Weiner, M. (1995). Discourse of race, nation and empire in pre-1945 Japan. Ethnic and Racial Studies, 18(3), pp. 433-456.

(42) Disch, R. & Schwartz, B. (1970). White discrimination (2nd ed.). New York: Dell.

(43) Capponi, N. (1993). The neuroses of the west; la nevrosi; dell 'occidente. Religioni e Societa, 8(16), pp. 22-30.

(44) Bullough, V. (1988). Historical perspective. Journal of Social Work and Human Sexuality, 7(1), pp. 15-24.

(45) Clark, K. & Clark, M. (1947). Racial self identification and preference in negro children. Newcomb & Hartly (eds.). Readings in Social Psychology, New York, Holt.

(46) Gould, K. (1984). Original works of Freud on women: social work references. Social Casework, 65(2), pp. 94-101.

(47) Rojek, C. (1986). The 'subject' in social work. Brtish Journal of Social Work, 16(1), pp. 65-77.

(48) Bullough, V. (1988). Historical perspective. Journal of Social Work and Human Sexuality, 7(1), pp. 15-24.

(49) Gaines, S. & Reed, E. (1995). Prejudice: from Allport to DuBois. American Psychologist, 50(2), pp. 96-103.

(50) Forbes, J. (1993). African and Native Americans. Urbana, Univ of Illinois Press.

(51) Kitano, H. (1985). Race Relations. Englewood Cliffs, NJ: Prentice-Hall.

(52) Stember, C. (1976). Sexual Discrimination. New York: Elsevier Scientific.

(53) Mazumdar, S. (1989). Racist Response to Discrimination: The Aryan Myth and South Asians in the US. South Asia Bulletin, 9(1), pp. 47-55.

(54) Wong, A. (1979). The Contest to Become Top Banana: Chinese Students at Canadian Universities, Canadian Ethnic Studies, 11(2), pp. 63-69.

(55) Hernton, C. (1965). Sex and Discrimination in America. New York: Grove.

(56) Haley, A. (1992). The Autobiography of Malcolm X. New York, Ballantine Books.

II

In A Global Sense

Western racism as defined in the global sense is regarded as an extension of "white supremacy" (1). Scholars of the social sciences study in great detail the implications that result in various forms of denigration. They trace the origins of drug addiction, hypertension, stress, family disjointure, and other societal ills to denigration (2). Fresh perspectives have not been forthcoming. Perhaps an attempt to add insight can be managed by ignoring, for the moment, the supremacy model and addressing its existence as a global form of bias in the perpetuation of Western culture.

Norm criteria by domination is a modern day manifestation of power extended from the aftermath of conquest and colonization, i.e.: racism. Racism according to Banton (3), refers to the efforts of a dominant group to exclude a dominated group from sharing in the material and symbolic rewards of society. It differs from other forms of exclusion in that qualification is based upon skin color and other observable physiological traits. Such traits are taken to suggest the inherent superiority of the dominant group, which is then rationalized as a natural order of the norm universe (4).

In 1944 W. E. B. DuBois wrote of the "Double Consciousness" (5). Double Consciousness is a theoretical construct that characterizes assimilation in Western nations. In brief it suggests that Asian-Americans maintained one set of behaviors appropriate within the group and another for the mainstream population into which they were required to assimilate. The purpose of assimilating was to realize their aspirations and ultimately a better life. In some cases "passing" for Euro-American—where a person of color would take on a dominant group identity in order to take advantage of the privileges and opportunities brought about by successful assimilation—was used. This was not a desire on the part of dark-skinned people to denigrate themselves, but rather a necessity of survival. Double Consciousness allowed for a degree of function to the extent that victims assumed another identity, but it was ultimately pathological because it required them to accept racist notions regarding dark skin. It promoted psychological pain in that it is a game that forced those who played it to be constantly on guard. It may also have required separation from family members, which is perhaps the most painful act of all. The pathology is potent for the psyche because family is where the sense of identity originates. Chestang referred to this as the "nurturing environment" (6). The "nurturing environment" can be compared to Erikson's "significant others: Those closest and most involved in the determination of an individual's sense of identity" (7). The individual's experiences and sense of identity growing out of his or her relationship with "significant others" play an important role in global existence and the ability of the individual to live a sane, productive, and, most importantly healthy life.

Mead's concept of the "generalized other" can also be used to assess global existence (8). Mead defined the generalized other as taking on the attitude of the wider society in regard to oneself, i.e. Asian-Americans taking on the attitudes of Euro-Americans. In this way, one learns to become an object to oneself, to have an identity, to know oneself through role taking and from the reflection of others. In acting out the roles of others, children discover that the roles belong to their own nature and begin to know themselves. From the many roles assumed, there gradually arises a generalized other. This attitude of the generalized other or organized community gives unity of self to individuals as they incorporate society's responses and react accordingly.

Mead spoke only of one generalized other. However, Asian-Americans who assume the attitude of the generalized other of the dominant group have a strong possibility of seeing themselves denigrated, as in fact they often are. The more they incorporate a racist image into their identity, the more they are enabled to act such racism out. Yet it is apparent that Asian-Americans do attain a good sense of self. It can then be assumed that there is an alternative generalized other, which Norton refers to as a "Dual Perspective" (9).

The alternative generalized other is the attitude of the family and immediate community environment, the "nurturing environment" of Chestang, the "significant others" of Erikson. If Asian-Americans receive love and care from their families, this can instill a positive notion of self. Since many are reasonably isolated from the dominant community physically and socially, at least early on, the attitude of the more immediate generalized other, the family, can develop, restore, or help them maintain self-esteem. They can use it as a buffer against the effects of the attitude of the generalized other from the dominant society as they experience the wider global community. This cannot be accomplished totally though, for they are very aware of the attitude of the dominant generalized other. The attempt is made more difficult in today's age of advanced media technology and urban living. If the mechanisms of socialization in the nurturing environment or the more immediate generalized other are positive, it may help Asian-Americans balance the destructive images that may come from the global Western population.

Of all the physical dimensions characteristic of the West's diverse population, racism is most enabled by the sight of skin color (10). Without sight, skin color cannot be perceived while its implications may still be apparent. Considering the function of skin, light skin has no fundamental dimension that dark skin does not have. Light skin has no fundamentally distinct superiority that would set it apart from dark skin. Yet, the global experience of Asians in the West based upon whether they are dark or light-

skinned is fundamentally different (11). It is the racist denigration of dark skin and the notion of light skin superiority that has
made a difference.

Those people of color socialized under the rubric of colonization do in fact discriminate. Their discrimination is a consequence
of having inculcated Euro norms emotionally and psychologically.
For South Americans the social and economic impact of skin color
is potent. The history of Afro-Nicaraugans of coastal Nicaragua is
a microcosm of that part of the continent. It has been suggested
by scholars that the original colonial Afro community saw themselves as the descendants of British civilization. They spoke English and idealized Anglo-Saxon—Euro—values and cultural practices. They perceived themselves as British subjects. In this context they began to refer to themselves as Creoles, mixed persons, to
connote their proximity to the British master race. They believed
themselves superior to the indigenous locals as a consequence of
being closer to the British skin color norm.

The Creole community in Nicaragua prospered and rose to a
position of economic and political eminence during the mid-nine-
teenth century. By the end of that century, they had been economically subjugated by North Americans and politically by the
indigenous population.

At the onset of the twentieth century Nicaragua's coast
economy was booming. Peasants migrated there to work as labor-
ers on the rubber and banana plantations. A second wave of Afros
were brought in from Jamaica, the Caymans, San Andres, and the
southern U.S. (12). They were mostly unskilled or semi-skilled
workers of almost pure African descent. The Creoles, already established on the Atlantic coast, were landowners, professional
people, artisans and fishermen, as well as functionaries in the new
North American enterprises. In short, they were of a higher class
than the immigrant Afros. They were also lighter-skinned. On the
basis of these and other differences, both groups of Afro descent
were considered distinct.

The social-cultural-racial distinction between these groups was maintained until recently. As late as the 1930s this issue was discussed by outside observers (13). With time, however, after a process of miscegenation, the two groups were transformed into one—the people who today are known as Creoles.

In their more than 300 years of existence on the Atlantic coast, Afro-Nicaraguans have experienced a unique ethnic odyssey. They started out as slaves, dark-skinned and the lowest of possible positions in the racist colonial hierarchy. They transformed their culture and language to the point where they denied their African origins. They became the elite of society. With the arrival of "lighter as brighter" via colonization they dropped from their lofty position to a middle one, where they have languished for 75 years. This odyssey is the key to understanding the contemporary Creole identity and its future evolution.

Light skin is an important indicator of Creole status. People of African descent in Nicaragua are usually Creole. However, there are many Miskitu, Mestizos, and Garifunas who share this same trait, and a substantial number of Creoles who do not (14). In general, light skin is recognized by Creoles as being characteristic of their group. However, many do not accept their mutual historical African origins. This is particularly true of the older generation, and stems from the historic identification with the European and North American colonizers. This limits Creole identification with other people of color. A contradiction exists, however, between the perceptions held by most Creoles of class and their actual situation. By major industrial standards they are poor. The Creole illusion of "high class" is derived from a romanticized collective memory of the past, a psychological identification with their colonizers and their position of relative affluence in comparison with the poverty of the rest of the coastal population is readily apparent.

Many studies have suggested that what existed in Nicaragua is typical for people of color in both North and South America. All are quite sensitive to issues involving skin color. Aware of racism once they reach the U.S. mainland, particularly light-skinned

Puerto Ricans may reject identification with people of color ada-mantly. Data collected from Mexicans, Mexican-Americans, Span-ish-speaking Americans, and Euro-American subjects in recent decades have verified high rejection rates toward all African-Ameri-cans. That rejection is most prominent among Mexican-Ameri-cans living in rural areas.

According to James Baldwin, the root of Western difficulty is directly related to skin color (15). This would contradict much of the rhetoric of the 1960s. But, as Hall notes, the issue of skin color was never resolved, merely relegated underground (16). Thus, a well-known phenomenon among dominated Asian groups is a re-jection of group membership (17). Internalizing alien norms is but one manner of expressing such rejection. For example, Asian-American women characterized by Caucasian features have more social status regardless of occupational skill or intellect (18). The resulting skin color hierarchy is arguably racist.

The global preference for light skin necessitated that it be-come an ideal of self-concept, even though light skin among some Asian-American groups is less common than the relative dark (19). Value-laden folk terms evolved among people of color that reflected that fact, such as "high-yellow," "ginger," "cream-colored," and "bronze" (20). When the term "black" was used, it more often inferred something derogatory.

The rhetoric of the 1960s espoused more conducive norms in the global community (21). Dark features were even heralded as desirable among some. In retrospect, however, what was practiced personally did not always coincide with what was espoused. Dark-skinned persons could be accepted, but there did not appear to be real progress. Still, the issue of skin color was seldom discussed publicly.

In their environment today, people of color are particularly aware of the impact skin color may derive (22). According to Neal and Wilson it has a different affect because physical appearance is important (23). In a relevant study Sciara had earlier found first-year college students devalued dark-skinned persons (24). Rank ordering of mean scores implied a strong pattern of negative appraisal assigned to dark-skinned Americans.

Among Asian-Americans the skin color issue is then a consequence of global domination by Europeans (25). Resultant domination encouraged their application of racist ideals indiscriminately. The uppermost in status among them became those whose color approximates that of the dominant group and the least being an opposite extreme. Conquered and in an effort to circumvent humiliation, Asian-Americans residing in Western nations accommodated the denigration of self. In the aftermath, a system was put in place that was not only physiologically alien but psychologically brutal. It resembles the configuration of a hierarchy. Under the circumstances the darkest encounter acute instances of bias reflected in hypergamy (26).

The latest trend in global bias is perpetrated by women of African descent residing in Western societies. Such persons in general, despite their being victims, are not immune to engaging racist acts (27). That fact was recently called to attention at prestigious Brown University, located in Providence, R.I., in the United States. There, an African-American male named Ralph Johnson and a Euro-American coed named Rachel Davidson caused a stir among African-American women on campus. The couples' private decision to date one another resulted in a "wall of shame" list written by African-American coeds—a list of African-American men who date Euro-American women (28). The fact that neither member of the couple engaged in any form of activity that would merit such harassment seemed irrelevant. Euro-American males who took part in similar activities thirty years ago would today have been expelled from campus with support of the entire academic community (29). The fact that perpetrators today are victims themselves should warrant no less tolerance (30). For people of color to publicly object when couples make a personal decision to date irrespective of race is a form of racism fashioned to suit the objectives of the racist. Whether the perpetrator be Euro-American or African-American is irrelevant.

Akin to the issue of racial discrimination in the post-colonial era is then a global skin color bias. In a global context, discrimination on the basis of race is questionable considering methodological grounds. Succinctly put, the issue of discrimination in a global context will be more contingent upon skin color in the post-colonial era. Skin color will allow for deviations from race and similar constructs deemed less relevant. The aforementioned is best illustrated via analogy.

An Asian- and Euro-American are obviously similar in genetic structure: both frequent a common existential space, and both rely upon nourishment from the environment of that space to evolve. But their environmental evolution within that space may differ significantly: for Asian-Americans, skin color is a critical aspect of life, whereas for Euro-Americans, though relevant, it is all but totally inconsequential (31). In human genes, as in social development, populations may have much in common, but otherwise descend from a distinct evolutionary heritage.

Thus, analysis of commonality in some respects may co-exist with contrasts in others. As pertains to Asian-Americans in a global context, persons who would equate discrimination with race independent of skin color in the post-colonial era would be in error. The most significant consequence of this error has been a subsequent tendency to underestimate the impact of skin color because an analogous impact does not pertain to Euro-Americans. As a result, the study of Asian-Americans is less accurate because it neglects skin color in lieu of race. In the hyper-utilization of race, Asian-Americans are then in effect dismissed from among those who would perpetuate discrimination. That dismissal ultimately derives and sustains pathologies among dark-skinned populations worldwide (32).

Global variations in human skin color is a fact of biological existence. Such variations are also a factor in the viability of human coexistence. Thus, in the aftermath of European colonization global sovereignties of diverse national backgrounds are predisposed to discrimination. Said discrimination is the result of an association of light skin with power. Assuming power is germane to human coexistence, understanding the implications of skin color is then compulsory to the fair and equitable negotiation of global outcomes. This had mattered historically for Semites because what ultimately matters in the context of skin color is that the Semitic skin color varies. For those among Semites who were inhabitants of the Arabian desert, from whence the Semites came, a remarkable racial homogeneity exists. It could therefore be logically concluded that though there is strictly no such thing as a Semitic race, Semites were in fact originally an ethnic group. Their cohesion in ancient times was strengthened by homogeneity as pertained to the wider "Oriental" type. That being no longer true in the post-colonial era accommodates differentiation vis-à-vis a world dominated by Europeans whose light skin is presumed the norm.

The events of ancient history led to a cultural chasm between the peoples of Semitic origin. This chasm was impacted by economic and political forces, which dispersed them into different lands and different situations. To the north of the Arabian desert, the Akkadians, settling into Mesopotamia, found peoples of a different origin and arguably of superior culture. Immediately, they assimilated the social, literary and artistic forms of these people. In another instance dark-skinned Ethiopians truncated themselves from the Semitic world and became more acclimated to the African continent (33). Only the Arabs, by their desert isolation, were sufficiently homogeneous enough to maintain a consistency of phenotype. Thus, among the Semitic type, dissimilarity prevails. The issue is further complicated by a contradiction of a racial group coincident with the Semitic language group. Accordingly, the two racial types described are not confined to the Semitic area. In fact the Oriental type extends to Iran and North Africa—the Armenoid to the Caucasus mountains. Conversely, they are not indigenous to all Semitic locations. Furthermore, in Abyssinia dark-skinned Ethiopians establish the existence of a distinct racial type of their own that has not discouraged Western racism.

To its credit, Israel today is one of the few post-colonial sovereignties where true ethnic diversity exists. Perhaps more than any other culture, it encompasses a rich mixture of skin colors, languages, and religions (34). Unfortunately, what is to its credit has also caused problems. Increased diversity has led to discrimination by the various factions for the conduct of policy on the basis of being light- or dark-skinned (35). Different languages and religions contribute to the tension, but the color of skin is by far the most potent factor.

The darkest in skin color among Jewish Semites is arguably the Beta Israel or Ethiopian Jews, sometimes referred to as Black Jews or Falasha (36). They do not "look Jewish" nor do they pretend to look Jewish. Many of the women have intermarried with tribes of varied skin colors—some Hamitic and some Semite. Opinions as to their migration to Israel are varied. But some insist that discrimination pertaining to the color of their skin is a major source of conflict. In fact, Ethiopian Semites in Israel are in more danger than those lighter-skinned from the Soviet Union.

Assisted by Israeli Semites in the spring of 1979 and early 1980, the American Association for Ethiopian Jews unified significant numbers of Ethiopian Semites with their families in Israel (37). The organizations worked with Christians in Ethiopia and Ethiopian Semites in Israel to substantiate the authenticity of the persons who were rescued. However, matters grew tense when an Israeli Jewish agency threatened the association. Pressure from other Jewish organizations and several United States senators in 1980 convinced the Jewish Agency to implement a family unification program much like the one developed by the American Association for Ethiopian Jews. Tensions were relieved after the various factions agreed to cooperate. The co-op was a successful strategy. A considerable number of Ethiopian Semites joined their families in Israel. However, Israel remained reluctant to permit migration of Ethiopian Semites for a number of reasons. Emigration was opposed by the late Emperor Haile Selassie until 1974. It was not until 1975 that the Law of Return satisfied the Israeli government opposition to entry of dark-skinned Ethiopians. There remains today an unspoken resignation in Israel to the migration of Ethiopian Semites associated with a pattern of color bias so indicative of modern post-colonial sovereignties (38).

"Brown Jews," or Beni Israel non-European Jews as they are called, reside for the most part near Bombay in Rangoon, Calcutta, and Malabar, India (39). Their skin color is a shade of brown and their features look more like those of Hindus rather than the typical Semite. Even so, Brown Jews state emphatically that they are in no way a product of Hindu miscegenation. Brown Jews divide themselves into two distinct castes: "black" and "white." Caste intermarriage is vehemently opposed. Many among the white caste—Gora—are darker in skin color than those of the black caste, but insist upon the "white" terminology nevertheless. Poverty and the extreme heat of the Indian climate over the years is the accepted rationale for their complexions having darkened.

White Jews maintain numerous methods of separating themselves. Inferior Jews such as black Jews are not allowed to touch white Jew kitchen utensils and are served ritualistic wine only after white Jews have been served. While relations between the two groups in India today appear cordial, the lines of demarcation in this male dominated society remain ever poised for group confrontation. Ultimately this substantiates the fact that, within each global sovereignty, differences of opinion exist regarding skin color. When decisions are made, the populations of light-skinned nations and the light-skinned within those nations wield more power than nations populated by dark-skinned groups; opinions of the former will be assumed to be heard and acted upon with greater urgency (40). However, in a post-colonial era efforts have been complicated by the emergence of the previously colonized latter onto the global body-politic. The ensuing dynamics contribute to an adversarial relationship between more powerful light-skinned populations and the less powerful dark-skinned in their efforts to negotiate global issues (41). The ensuing discrimination tests the viability of global coexistence. As dark-skinned nations feel more inclined to sit as equals, post-colonial sovereignties feel morally

obliged to accommodate them. However, despite moral obligation
the existence of skin color bias is the emerging source of conflict
that will evolve unchecked as long as race is definitive of social
issues.

In the heart of Africa, Ethiopia is historically significant. It
covers a geographical area of about 1.2 million square kilometers
(42). Accurate census information pertaining to Ethiopia's people
is questionable, therefore, what does exist may be subject to a large
margin of error. Given said circumstances, up until 1975 the population of Ethiopia was estimated to be 2,102,000 (43). More recent figures have been less available for a variety of reasons indicative of less developed countries. However, Ethiopia is a nation characterized by contrasts. Among its people, more than seventy languages and over 200 dialects are spoken. It encompasses the world's
three major religions: Christianity, Islam, and Judaism.

Ethiopia has never existed without tension between the various religious and language groups. Following the 1974 Revolution, a right to self-determination for all nationalities was acknowledged by the Programme of National Democratic Revolution thus
ending domination of one nationality by another. A socialist military government in Ethiopia made an earnest attempt to carry out
such policies. It utilized a diversity of popular languages and pro-
claimed Muslim holidays as public holidays, etc. It extended respect to the lesser cultural factions thereby further validating their
intentions as honorable. Finally, by allowing greater local autonomy
the government had hoped to sustain harmony for Ethiopia's future.

The changes brought about in Ethiopia had little impact upon
the quality of life. Without respect for laws and policy, Semites
were denigrated in Ethiopian culture by societal structure. In every phase of society their status sustained differentials in amounts
of power, prestige, benefits, obligations, and rights. The status of
Semites refers, therefore, to the collection of different positions
that they hold and carry the force of cultural norm and/or more.
Any deviations from such norms would result in consequences as

swift and harsh as those of law. It all culminates to reduce Semites to worthless objects of domination that predisposes them to Western migration.

As per domination, the darker skin of Ethiopian Semites necessitates their status in the West as inferior. Their most salient feature being skin color may have an effect upon every phase of their lives including self-concept. It is a "master status" that distinguishes them as inferior—particularly among anti-semites. So potent is this "master status" that it is frequently grounds for social discourse between persons of light and dark skin color but who belong to the same ethnic group (44). A resort to belligerence is an indication that, for some among the dark-skinned, life has been particularly stressful given the psychologically conflicting implications in Western society. That is, Ethiopian Semites have internalized much of Western culture, but, unlike European Semites, cannot structurally assimilate into it (45). Their willingness to idealize light skin as the norm regardless reflects an effort not to denigrate themselves but to improve their quality of life. In so doing, Ethiopian Semites may develop disdain for dark skin because the disdain is a by-product of colonization. It is regarded by Western institutions as an obstacle that might otherwise afford Ethiopian Semites the opportunities necessary to succeed. For those who labor, unaware of the inherent limitations, lower self-esteem is the end result. In order to reduce resultant stress some have opted in various ways to compensate for their dark skin color. Furthermore, since class and quality of life closely correlates with having a color approximate to the dominant population norm, light skin has emerged as critical to a healthy Ethiopian self-concept.

The normalization of light skin by Ethiopian Semites adheres to the dictates of Western culture. Such persons may migrate, bringing with them notions pertaining to light skin that exacerbate negative ideas regarding dark skin. In Israel, Euro-Semites who begin the assimilation process harbor the belief that light skin is superior and dark skin denotes inferiority. This then imposes upon their ability to assimilate with others, particularly of Ethiopian descent.

American sociological studies are replete with the analysis of skin color, perhaps due to the heterogeneous nature of Western cultures. In an effort to assimilate, Ethiopian Semites in Israel are considered inferior and/or "minorities" by virtue of skin color—when relatively dark. The social science literature, for the most part, has ignored their quest, being primarily concerned with European Semites. Any reference to norms are then constructed from the dimensions of a Eurocentric model. Thus, while Ethiopian Semites have increased contact with their Euro-Israeli counterpart, scrutiny of skin color has escaped scientific analysis (46). This distorts Ethiopian self-concept by domination and extends to the acceptance of alien norms implying the ability of the dominant group to impose their norms absent consideration for the latter's reaction. This is because, regardless of the particular methods used, those who dominate may define the norm universe in their best interest. Furthermore, aside from the more obvious aggressive tactics, true dominance may derive from influential behavior and relative status. In Israel, European Semites are in a position to exercise dominance over Ethiopian Semites tainted by the stigma of dark skin (47). Euro-Semites may act out their dominance in the context of norms without ever making conscious or overt gestures. Much of their appeal takes root in the cultural prescriptions of everyday life. Given the status differential between Euro and Ethiopian Semites, resulting perceptions of the dark-skinned are then tantamount to denigration.

Inasmuch as racism is endemic to global existence, among people of color, third world solidarity is a myth. The experience of European conquest and/or domination in the wake of self-deprecating ideals has compromised any potential for solidarity. Dark-skinned Americans by virtue of skin color are a contradiction to Euro domination. Vehement forms of racism are visited in their ability to threaten the Euro gene pool. However, the notion of racism among Asian-Americans is no less pathological than racism directed at them. Consequently, scholars who study global issues have facilitated the trivialization of skin color discrimination without engaging significant debate or empirical analysis. In a loosely organized conspiracy, to do so, they retort, would be polemic and demean scientific methods. Their hegemony is neither justifiable nor ethical, but a pseudo-scientific collaboration designed to determine the existential reality of global human life. In the aftermath, the skin color discrimination experienced and perpetuated by people of color is all but dismissed from what is existentially real. Their inability to conform to the Eurocentric experience is a casualty of the hegemony that to date has canonized race. Such an inductive method undermines democracy and discourages the intellectual rigor that could provide new solutions to global problems in the post-colonial era. In a time vastly more diverse than in the past, consequences will court disaster.

In any non-totalitarian society, certain views necessarily dominate others, just as certain movements are more influential than others; manifestation of this global tendency is recapitulated by the manner in which discrimination has been characterized. The dynamics enabling it are compulsory to the comprehension of global issues in the new millennium. As an ideology, race is covertly associated with discrimination because it is an extension of Eurocentric hegemony. Race versus skin color necessitates an unspoken, collective "us" against "them" among members of the academy. Extended from that belief is thus subjugation of contrasting views. Such subjugation overrides the possibility that a more skeptical, independent thinker might conclude otherwise.

Lastly, skin color, being centrifugal to discrimination in the global sense, helps Asian-Americans determine their existential reality (48). Their role in that determination must include the decoding of race based concepts, illumination of hegemonic inequalities, and other moves to intellectual discourse. Via the prescripts of struggle, their efforts have not been ahistorical. Those toils are not without precedent but, in fact, endure as a continuum wedded to the larger post-colonial construct. Enabled by the illumination of skin color in lieu of race, scholars will contribute to an effort to purge race from the global ethos of social issues. The aftermath will make a significant contribution to the study of discrimination despite the prevalence of post-colonial impediments.

References

(1) Kitano, H. (1985). Race relations. Englewood Cliffs, NJ: Prentice-Hall.

(2) Beckett, A. K.,(1983). The relationship of skin color to blood pressure among Black Americans. Unpublished master's theses, Atlanta University, Atlanta.

(3) Kitano, H. (1985). Race relations. Englewood Cliffs, NJ: Prentice-Hall.

(4) Minor, N. & McGauley, L. (1988). A different approach: dialogue in education. Journal of Teaching in Social Work, 2(1), pp. 127-140.

(5) Myrdal, G. (1944). An American dilemma. New York: Harper & Row.

(6) Bates, M. (1983). Using the environment to help the male skid row alcoholic. Social Casework, 64(5), 276-282.

(7) Erickson, E. (1968). Identity, youth and crisis. Norton. New York, N.Y.

(8) Mead, G. (1934). Mind, Self and Society. University of Chicago Press, Chicago, IL.

(9) Norton, D. (1993). Diversity, early socialization, and temporal development: The dual perspective revisited. Social Work. January, Vol 38(1), 82-90.

(10) Hall, R. E. (1990). The projected manifestations of aspiration, personal values, and environmental assessment cognates of cutaneo-chroma (skin color) for a selected population of African-Americans. University Microfilms International, Ann Arbor, MI, 1-192.

(11) Kitano, H. (1985). Race relations. Englewood Cliffs, NJ: Prentice-Hall.

(12) Lancaster, R. (Oct 1991). Skin color, race and racism in Nicaragua. Ethnology, 30, 4, 339-353.

(13) Ibid

(14) Ibid

(15) Jones, B. F. (1966). James Baldwin: The struggle for identity. British Journal of Sociology, 17, 107-121.

(16) Hall, R. E. (1995). The Bleaching Syndrome: African Americans' Response to Cultural Domination vis-a-vis Skin Color. Journal of Black Studies, 26 (2), pp. 172-183.

(17) Banerjee, S. (1985). Assortive mating for color in Indian Population. Journal of Bioscience, 17, pp. 205-209.

(18) Okazawa-Rey, M., Robinson, T., & Ward, J. V. (1987). Black women and the politics of skin color and hair. Women and therapy, 6(1/2), 89-102.

(19) Hall, R. E. (1995). The Bleaching Syndrome: African Americans' Response to Cultural Domination vis-a-vis Skin Color. Journal of Black Studies, 26 (2), pp. 172-183.

(20) Herskovits, M. (1968). The American Negro. Bloomington: Indiana University Press.

(21) Herod, C. (1995). New day in Babylon: The Black power movement and American culture, 1965-1975. Canadian Review of Studies in Nationalism, 22(1-2), pp. 178-179.

(22) Hertel, B., & Hughes, M. (1988). The significance of color remains. Social Forces, 68, 1105-1120.

(23) Neal, A. M., & Wilson, M. L. (1989). The role of skin color and features in the Black community: Implications for Black women and therapy. Clinical Psychology Review, 9, 323-333.

(24) Sciara, F. J. (1983). Skin color and college student prejudice. College Student Journal, 17, 390-394.

(25) Kim, K. (1990). Blacks Against Korean Merchants: An Interpretation of Contributory Factors. Migration World Magazine, 18(5), 11-15.

(26) Hall, R. (1997). Eurogamy among Asian-Americans: A note on Western assimilation. The Social Science Journal, 34(3), pp. 403-408.

(27) Hall, R. (1992). Bias among African Americans regarding skin color: Implications for social work practice, Research on Social Work Practice, 2(4), 479-86.

(28) Gose, B. (1996, May). Public debate over a private choice. Chronicle of Higher Education, pp. A45, A47.

(29) Wolf, C. (1992). Constructions of a lynching. Sociological Inquiry, 62(1), pp. 8397.

(30) Hall, R. E. (1995). The Bleaching Syndrome: African Americans' Response to Cultural Domination vis-a-vis Skin Color. Journal of Black Studies, 26 (2), pp. 172-183.

(31) Frost, P. (1988). Human skin color: A possible relationship between its sexual dimorphism and its social perception. Perspectives in Biology and Medicine, 32(1), 38-58.

(32) Arroyo, J. (1996). Psychotherapist bias with Hispanics: An analog study. Hispanic Journal of Behavioral Sciences, 18(1), 21-28.

(33) Barton, G. (1934). Semitic and Hamitic origins, social and religious by George Aaron Barton. University of Pennsylvania Press, Philadelphia, Pa.

(34) Ashkenazi, M. & Wein, A. (1983). Ethiopian immigrants in Beer-Sheeva. Highland Park, Ill.: American Association for Ethiopian Jews.

(35) Henik, A., Munitz, S., & Priel, B. (1985). Color, skin color preferences and self color identification among Ethiopian and Israeli-born children. Israeli Social Science Research, 3, 74-84.

(36) Yilmah, S. (1996). From Falasha to Freedom. Genfen Pub. House: Hewlett, N.Y.

(37) Ibid

(38) Foulkes, R. (1994). Hortense Powdermaker's after freedom: Making sense of the conundrum of Black/Jewish relations in American anthropology and society. Western Journal of Black Studies, 18(4), 231-243.

(39) Barton, G. (1934). Semitic and Hamitic origins, social and religious by George Aaron Barton. University of Pennsylvania Press, Philadelphia, Pa.

(40) Huth, P. (1998). Major Power Intervention in International Crises, 1918-1988. Journal of Conflict Resolution, 42(6), 744-770.

(41) Keohane, R. & Nye, J. (1971). Transnational Relations and World Politics. Cambridge: Harvard University Press.

(42) Haile, D. (1980). Law and the status of women in Ethiopia. African Training and Research Center for Women. Addis Ababa University. Ababa, Ethiopia.

(43) Ibid

(44) Morrow vs the Internal Revenue Service, 742 F. Supp. 670 (N.D. Ga. 1990).

(45) Wagenheim, K. & deWagenheim, O. (1973). The Puertorriqenos. Garden City, Doubleday.

(46) Fujino, D. (1993). Extending exchange theory: Effects of ethnicity and gender on Asian American heterosexual relationships. Dissertation Abstracts International, 53(9-B).

(47) Chan, C. (1987). Asian America women: Psychological responses to sexual exploitation and cultural stereotypes. Asian American Psychological Association Journal 12(1), 11-15.

(48) Hall, R. (2001). Filipina Eurogamy: Skin color as vehicle of psychological colonization. Manila, Philippines: Giraffe Books.

III

Racism via Skin Color

The imposition of racism upon the post-colonial world order extends to the behavioral norms of not a few Western societies. Without exception, racism is a social force that impairs the ability of Asians to migrate to and/or assimilate in America. Furthermore, in an effort to divert attention from the atrocities of racism scholars have diluted the rhetoric of social justice to include religion, ancestry, age, sex, sexual orientation, gender identity, disability, place of birth, etc. (1). Yet in America—and despite rhetoric to the contrary—racism persists. Although literature acknowledges racism among the list of societal pathologies, amidst augmentation of issues it has been all but institutionalized (2). Greater focus on its global aspects would enhance the self-esteem of Asian-Americans and enable the elimination of oppression in toto. Instead, discussions of racism rely too heavily upon what transpires between African- and Euro-Americans as a means of circumventing controversy. In the outcome, Asian-Americans are cast as victims without a voice. Rather than asking how they might eliminate racism in toto, the American intelligentsia asks nebulous questions, such as: What are the means to racial harmony? In what ways can they eliminate racism without stirring controversy? Finally, what are the consequences for those who characterize racism using the black/white dichotomy?

From the backdrop of these queries emerge consequences for the adversaries of racism. The ability of Asian-Americans to assimilate will require America to construct a more encompassing view of racism. In an effort to accomplish the aforementioned, it is necessary to begin discussions of racism in a more encompassing context. Asian-Americans, and other people of color, have been more than just victims of racism. Thus, as an alternative to the traditional black/white dichotomy view of racism, focus upon racism and skin color is put forth as a more appropriate and global model for analyzing Asian-Americans in the post-colonial era.

Migration patterns provide unique insight to the Asian-American experience. According to the OECD, migration to Western nations including Germany, Netherlands, United Kingdom, Australia, Canada, and the United States account for a significant portion of the total populations (3). Table 1 illustrates the percentage of foreigners in each of the stated countries in 1996; Table 2 illustrates the number of foreigners by thousands who sought asylum in 1996/1997; and Table 3 illustrates percentage of people of color who migrated by selected countries in 1997.

Table 1: % of Foreigners

Nation	% of Population
Germany	8.9
Netherlands	4.4
United Kingdom	3.4
Australia	21.1
Canada	17.4
United States	9.3

Table 2: Foreigners Seeking Asylum (1000s)

Nation	Asylum seek 1000s
Germany	104.4
Netherlands	34.4
United Kingdom	41.5
Australia	7.7
Canada	23.9
United States	79.8

Nation	Table 3 % Who Migrate Migrants of Color	Percent
France	Morocco	12%
	Turkey	06%
	Algeria	14%
Germany	Turkey	10%
United Kingdom	India	06%
United States	Philippines	06%
	Mexico	18%
	Dominican Rep	04%

As per tables 1-3 Australia is a Western nation with the largest foreign born population at 21.1%, followed by Canada at 17.4%. Germany has the largest number of asylum seekers in the thousands at 104.4, followed by the United States at 79.8. France has the largest percentage of people of color who migrate there at 32%, followed by the United States at 28%.

The desire among Asians to migrate West comes at the threat of life and death. In Dover, England, 58 Asians were found dead from suffocation after stowing away in an air-tight vessel. They had paid criminal elements to smuggle them into the country in hopes of seeking asylum and eventual integration. The inability of unskilled Asians to enter into states of the European Union has led to such desperate loss of life (4).

Racism has impeded the migration of Asians and other people of color into Western societies as an extension of colonial abominations (5). Volumes of literature have had little impact in facilitating its demise. In fact, racism is a psychosocial event perpetrated among people of color—including Asian-Americans—against their darkest-skinned brethren (6). About the accuracy of this assumption there should be no doubt. Notwithstanding, to characterize racism in a narrow "black/white" dichotomy does disservice to the scientific method. It enables the otherwise absurd rhetoric of hier-

archy within a single species. It provides a conduit for the continued worldwide social, economic, and political oppression of Asian
peoples. However deserving of sympathy, the role of victims cannot be ignored. While investigating their undertaking may not be
popular or "politically correct," to do so regardless is what distinguishes science from quackery (7).

A cursory review of the literature affirms a critical bias in the
analysis of racism (8). Not only are Euro-Americans and others in
the West consistently regarded as perpetrators but Asian-Americans and other people of color are consistently regarded as victims.
Nonetheless, via skin color, Asian-Americans contribute to the
perpetuation of racism (9). The emerging miscegenation among
an increasingly lighter-skinned, racially indistinct American population, requires dialogue addressing racism to move from discussions of "race" to that of skin color. Such a trait is germane to the
myth of third world solidarity (10). As perpetrators, Asian nations
have not acknowledged the consequences of their role (11). This
does not negate the pervasiveness of what Euro-Americans do, but
allows an amplified analysis to include all those involved.

In the post-colonial era persons of Asian descent became exotic "things" necessitating their status as "minorities" (12). By
European standards dark skin is their most socially potent and
salient feature because it contrasts with the Western mainstream
(13). Dark skin may have an effect upon every phase of Asian-
American life including mate selection, stereotype, treatment within
the judicial system, and most importantly self-concept (14). It is a
"master status" that differentiates Asian-Americans as an inferior
element of society (15). So potent is this "master status" that it has
recently served as grounds for litigation between persons of light
and dark skin color but who belong to the same ethnic group
(16). A resort to legal tactics is an indication that, for Asian-Americans, racism has been particularly painful given the psychologically conflicting implications of dark skin.

Thus, Asian-Americans have idealized Western culture, but
unlike Europeans are prohibited from structural assimilation into

it (17). Their willingness regardless reflects a desire not to devalue themselves but to improve their quality of life. In so doing, Asian-Americans developed a disdain for dark skin because the disdain is an aspect of Western culture (18). They recognize the preferences of various institutions. The logical outcome is disassociation from their darker-skinned brethren by denigration in an effort to succeed. For those who labor, unaware of the inherent limitations, failure is the end result. Furthermore, since quality of life closely correlates with having a color approximate to the Euro-American ideal, light skin has emerged as critical to the ability of Asian-Americans to assimilate (19). Thus, Western colonialism has predisposed Asian-Americans to the internalization of Euro-American ideals. In logic, their common experience with other people of color has fostered a sense of cohesion and solidarity. However, under the circumstances of post-colonial influences, third world solidarity is a myth manifested in little more than rhetoric. Accordingly, those of darkest skin have been subjected to various forms of racism less salient in the shadow of white racism.

As per Asian-Americans, the issue of skin color as pertains to racism has a long and established history (20). Asian migrants, such as Japanese, travel West with racist notions pertaining to light skin that exacerbate negative ideas regarding dark skin (21). When they begin the assimilation process, the belief that light skin is superior and dark skin denotes inferiority imposes upon their ability to interact with dark-skinned people (22). It may in fact have had much to do with the recent tensions between African and Asian-American communities in Los Angeles and various other parts of the U.S. (23).

The Asian perception of light skin is indicative of Asian groups in America and elsewhere abroad (24). The phenomenon is further dramatized by those who arrive from India bringing with them strict racial rankings of people on the basis of color (25). As a group notorious for endogamy, Indian Asians who marry out, unless they are dark-skinned, do so almost exclusively to persons of European descent (26). For Asian women, a desire to marry

Euro-American men is regarded as an invaluable asset (27). Idealization of Euro-American men qualifies such men as their spousal ideal. It further increases or reduces the frequency of exogamy with the various people of color (28). It also necessitates exogamy between Americans and Asian-Americans; having equal socioeconomic status is contingent upon the ability of the non-Asian via offspring to lighten the skin color and Westernize the features of their Asian counterpart. It is most apparent among foreign students who express a desire to migrate West. When the socioeconomic status between they and their potential spouses is unequal, an "exchange" theory based upon proximity to Euro-American genes will be used as the selection criterion (29). The darker the skin, the more will be required in exchange. This is true whether either of the couple is foreign or American.

While many Asian-Americans internalize racist notions idealizing light skin, there is exception. The Japanese in fact frequently think ill of Euro light skin (30). Identification with the historical "greatness" associated with Asian civilizations reinforces in Asian-Americans, who marry exogamously, assumptions concerning the racist ordering of people. Unfortunately, a high number of dark-skinned people are not well ranked (31). While some may think ill of Euro-Americans, Asians who migrate to America can hardly fail to note predominance of the Euro-American population within the mainstream of society (32).

Perhaps the most insidious manifestation of racism in the postcolonial era among Asian-Americans is referred to as "brown racism." According to Washington (33), brown racism is perpetrated by Mestizos, Chinese, Filipinos, and South Asians against persons of African descent. It is considered a variation of "white" racism that probably occurred as a result of colonial conquest and is most often reflected in the opinions of particularly recent Asian-American citizens and their views of African-Americans.

In an effort to deal with post-colonial issues, recent Asian-American migrants direct accusations of racism at their oppressed counterpart—particularly darker-skinned African-Americans—and all but ignore brutality of the status quo. This scenario is drama-tized in the controversial writings of Asian-American Ying Ma, in the aftermath of the brutal murder of Chinese-American Vincent Chin.

It is her contention that what is perceived as racism today completely misses the point. She criticizes President Clinton's "Race Initiative" panel for ignoring the real race problem between mi-nority populations. Of particular concern from her perspective is the hatred directed at Asian-Americans by African-Americans who reside in low-income neighborhoods of the inner-city. She draws upon her childhood experiences to reach these conclusions.

Ying Ma reportedly migrated from China at age ten. Her fam-ily settled in Oakland, California, where crime, poverty, and racial tension were prevalent. She felt out of place by the clothes she wore and her inability to speak English. Her classmates began calling her "Ching Chong," "China girl," and "Chow Mein." They degraded her culture, language, ethnicity, and race. In her typical Asian way, Ying Ma remained silent.

Eventually Ying Ma improved her command of the English language, but perhaps due to her cultural norm did not respond to verbal insults. Her trips to and from school were a constant effort to circumvent harassment. She endured many insults such as spit balls, profanity and shouts of "stupid Chinamen" on her bus ride home. The label "Chinaman" was applied to any persons who displayed an Asian appearance such as Vietnamese, Koreans, etc. Unlike the other Asians on the bus who tuned out the insults, Ying Ma took them personally and indicted an entire race of people in her adulthood by what she experienced as a child. The fact that light-skinned African-Americans, middle class African-Americans or other Americans suffered similar insults from the same group did not matter. Ying Ma used this opportunity to reach the first psychological milestone in her being non-violently colonized by her internalization of colonial psychic matter in the way she re-garded African-Americans.

Despite the oppression and racism that characterize any im-

ASIA COLOR QUEST   61

poverished inner-city neighborhood, Ying Ma grew increasingly bitter and outraged by African-Americans. She admits with a pride and arrogance that her fluency in English eventually surpassed that of those who had harassed her during childhood. This was her second psychological milestone in that her perception of African-Americans reflects the stereotype of their intellectual inferiority professed by Murray and other post-colonial intellectuals. What is more, she admits to being the object of vulgar sexual remarks, which, she contends, embarrassed her. This complaint about sexual vulgarities is another critical aspect of racism. It stems from rhetoric of the Antebellum where southern slave traders sought to demean African-Americans in their stereotype of the "black beast rapist," as if Euro-Americans were incapable of such behaviors.

Ying Ma was not only mindful of the insults hurled at her personally by African-American students but those hurled at other Asians as well. She recalls a middle-aged Chinese vendor in her high school cafeteria who spoke poor English. On a daily basis African-American students insulted him with shouts of "dumb Ching!" Ying Ma describes African-Americans who would approach elderly Asians to frighten them with taunts of: "Yee-ya, Ching-chong, ah-ee, un-yahhh!" She further takes issue with African-Americans who would insist that her people "go back to where you came from!" By the time she graduated high school and left inner-city Oakland, Ying Ma had been effectively colonized, not in her native homeland but by the post-colonial psychic matter that now dominated her perspective of an oppressed dark-skinned population.

Ying Ma was pleased to graduate high school because it gave her an opportunity to escape the "black animals" in inner-city Oakland. She enrolled at a college made beautiful by its distance from inner-city Oakland. Similar to those who had colonized her own people, Ying Ma had cooperated in the colonization of inner-city Oakland in that she only took from the community and gave nothing back (35). Today she continues to reminisce about what she refers to as "black racism." She recalls an African-American

HALL

woman shouting at a Korean man in a command of English obviously now inferior to her own: "You f—ing Chinese person! Didn't you hear that I asked you to move yo' ass? You too stupid to understand English or something?" Ying Ma was by now emotionally jaded and completely disinterested in the overarching dynamics that might have preceded such a confrontation.

In a colonized testimony, Ying Ma refers to Asians all across America who are experiencing what she went through as a child. She contemplates the stereotype of her own people—another manifestation of racism—as having language deficiencies, small size, and their enduring silence. Most of them, she assumes, will never escape the "black ghetto" for a beautiful "white" neighborhood far away. This makes them hate African-Americans whom, she contends, much of America refuses to acknowledge as capable of racism.

Commensurate with racism Ying Ma directs her criticisms at "prominent black leaders" who refuse to acknowledge the existence of "black racism." She refers to activists such as Al Sharpton and Jesse Jackson as if she were tutored by their political opponents. Even the world-renowned John Hope Franklin, African-American history scholar and chair of President Clinton's race panel, cannot escape her criticism. She insists that African-Americans such as Franklin complain continuously about racism inflicted by "whites" while completely ignoring that by African-Americans against innocent migrant Asian-Americans.

Ying Ma does not limit her attacks to African-Americans. In the spirit of subjugation, she criticizes the leadership of her Asian community as well. According to her, they have failed to act upon "black racism" because they fear African-Americans. Describing a rally she attended in New York's Chinatown, Ying Ma had gone to learn about Indonesia's history of discrimination against ethnic Chinese. That discrimination had recently resulted in a wave of bloody anti-Chinese riots. Then, without prompting, Ying Ma heard a woman at the rally begin to scream hysterically about her frustrations with African-American racism. The woman's name was

Mee Ying Lin. Mee Ying Lin had felt similar about African-Americans, as did she—she hated them. By then Ying Ma was certain that others had felt just as she: that African-Americans aside from being the victims of racism were perpetrators as well.

Ying Ma contends that the reason "black racism" is ignored is due to the fact that the Asian-American leadership is out of touch with the common Asian-American community. That disconnect is even more pronounced at the national level. A disproportionate representation of the Asian-American leadership consists of assimilated Asian-Americans whose families may have migrated to America several generations or sooner. They have a different perspective and different concerns compared to their more recent migrant counterparts. Furthermore, there may be class, language, and cultural differences that alienate Asian-American leadership from its not yet assimilated counterpart. Thus, they cannot know or understand the critical issues faced by recent migrants because they live comfortable middle-class lives. This disconnect encourages many Asian-Americans to then remain silent about "black racism."

In the context of colonization, Ying Ma is joined by other Asians who do not necessarily share her racist view of African-Americans. One such person was Rose Tsai. Ms. Tsai headed the San Francisco Neighbors Association and also ran as a candidate for a seat on the city's Board of Supervisors. According to Ms. Tsai, the typical Asian himself is not culturally prepared to defend against ghetto racism because "Asian culture is just not that confrontational...." Asian-Americans differ from African-Americans in that African-Americans will not hesitate to confront and fight for their rights. Asian-Americans on the other hand are so naïve about American politics that it is difficult for Asian-American leadership to get them to vote. This might explain the passivity of Asian migrants in the inner-city. In fact, this racist view of Asian-Americans does not coincide with reality. Organizations like the Asian American Legal Defense Fund, the National Asian-Pacific American Legal Consortium, and the Organization for Chinese Americans are

examples of Asian-American groups who are no more or less confrontational than any other Americans. Perhaps they are less vis-
ible because they do not fit the Asian stereotype. Unfortunately
Ying Ma and others criticize such groups, accusing them of having
ignored "black racism" and having chosen instead to focus their
attention on such events as the recent investigation of Asian do-
nors of illegal campaign funds and the Republican opposition in
Congress to Asian-American Bill Lann Lee's nomination as director of the Office of Civil Rights. From Ying Ma's perspective, such
issues are trivial.

Ying Ma is bent on condemning the Asian-American leadership who do not support racist views of African-Americans. She
further asserts that it is not a matter of an inability to confront
"black racism" but rather a decision not to do so. According to her,
some Asian-American leaders have even attempted to justify "black
racism" as a result of competition over limited resources. The most
glaring example is when Asian-American businesses locate in African-American neighborhoods. Boycotts like the 1990 year-long
stand-off between the African-American community and a Korean
store in Brooklyn inflamed both sides. Another example involved
Korean merchants and occurred in south-central Los Angeles during the 1992 Rodney King riots. While the riots were not directed
at Asian-Americans initially the violence soon spread to them, en-
gulfing their segregated community. Ultimately, Ying Ma does
not see the economic argument as relevant. It is instead, she contends, a smoke-screen for jealousy against Asian-Americans by African-Americans who view them as better off.

Socio-economic class eliminates any doubt according to Ying
Ma that "blacks" commit racist acts against Asian-Americans. In
the case of San Francisco's African-American dominated Hunter's
Point public housing, low-income Southeast Asian residents, who
are in the minority, have repeatedly encountered racial harassment.
Racist threats and destruction of property have occurred unchecked
for years to the point of almost becoming a norm. Ying Ma cites
Philip Nguyen, of the Southeast Asian Community Center, who

insists his community has made every effort to get along with and even befriend African-Americans to no avail. The problems have remained for ten years or more.

Under close observation, Ying Ma's argument is less formidable. There have been efforts on the part of those such as Joe Hicks, executive director of the Los Angeles City Human Relations Commission, to bring African- and Asian-Americans together. Such efforts unfortunately have failed. Accusations of racism, based on African-American's economic jealousy of Asian-American success, misses the point. That is not to say that economics are irrelevant, but the fact is if all other matters were equal between African- and Asian-Americans problems would remain. This notion approaches the crux of the matter, which Ying Ma and other Asian-Americans refuse to acknowledge in discussions of "black racism." Simply put, it is the particularly northern Asian—Japanese, Korean, Chinese—colonial sense of human hierarchy and Asian superiority that ranks all dark-skinned persons as inferior. Until that issue is addressed publicly, it will remain an unspoken but no less significant wedge between both communities.

In the spirit of colonization, Ying Ma acknowledges painstakingly that there is some Asian "prejudice" against African-Americans. However, her response is to trivialize it and all but dismiss it as being relevant to "black racism." After all, she muses Asian prejudices, cannot possibly be that significant because many Asian migrants had never even seen a "black" person before coming to America. Somehow Ying Ma's formidable intellect dismisses the popular sale of "darkie" toothpaste in Korea, the international criticism of Japan for their denigration of "black" people, and the comments by Japan's Prime Minister that African-Americans especially are a social problem. More importantly, Ying Ma dismisses historical Chinese culture, which demeaned everything Western and taught the young that all non-Chinese—particularly dark-skinned Africans—were barbarians. Subsequently, Asian-American migrants who had never seen a "black" person prior to coming to America considered them inferior. A cursory review of the research literature complies with this notion.

According to Hogue the most obvious indications of a skin color hierarchy among Asians exists in the attitudes of Northern Asians, including Chinese, Japanese, and Koreans (36). All three peoples have a significant degree of racial homogeneity within the population. Arguably, it is among the Japanese that the strongest evidence of bias may exist. Historically, they have maintained myths that rationalize the superiority of Japanese people as an aspect of cultural norm. Thus, their world is composed of the Japanese and their inferior foreign counterparts referred to as "ghigin." It should come as little surprise that this belief would be relevant to Japan's treatment of non-Japanese—particularly the dark-skinned. They were no less arrogant and brutal in their management of colonial subjects than the West (37). The Japanese color hierarchy is manifested in a strong sense of superiority, which they apply on the basis of skin color, ranking those darkest at the very bottom. The same system is applied to Japanese citizens who may be among Japan's minority group.

In the *Rape of Nanking,* author Iris Chang refers to the cruelty and brutality of the Japanese toward the Chinese during their colonial occupation (38). However, the Japanese and the Chinese are not so different in their regard for dark-skinned people. Like the Japanese, the Chinese have historically regarded themselves as superior, separate, and apart from the rest of mankind. Any non-Chinese are considered barbarians who would welcome the opportunity to stain the purity of Chinese blood. As a result, when Chinese students travel abroad to be educated, they are warned by their elders not to return married to a "red-haired devil" whom they do not perceive as human (39). So-called "red-haired devils" are of course light-skinned humans who hailed from the West. Those who are dark-skinned and/or from Africa occupy a rank so far below Western "devils" as not to even be considered worthy of Chinese's denigration. This was apparent in a recent rock-throwing incident of hundreds of Chinese students who descended unprovoked upon visiting African students to China (40).

In the interest of objectivity, the issue of color in China is much more complex than the American version over centuries. China did in fact assimilate Mongolian and Manchu invaders whom they regarded as barbaric. Furthermore, China also absorbed a population of minorities making the issue of bias in many ways confusing to non-Chinese observers. In their logic, to be superior is to be Chinese, which would create great difficulty for any foreigner. In contrast, Chinese living off the mainland in such places as Hong Kong participate actively in Western social affairs (41).

It is common knowledge among social scientists that the social distance between Euro- and Asian-Americans is minimal. What they have failed to consider is why that is true. Kuo-Shu, Pen-Hua, and Ching-Fang conducted a study on social distance using Chinese students (42). Their research was located at the National Taiwan University, Taipei, and Republic of China. The objective was to test subjects for their social distance attitudes toward 25 national and ethnic groups. They used a social distance scale, which was modified to be particularly applicable to Chinese students. The primary findings were: (a) The social distance attitudes of Chinese students varied for different national and ethnic groups. According to the mean social distance, persons with light skin occupied the highest status ranking and those with dark skin occupied the lowest. Politics were not irrelevant, especially recent events, to the tendency of discrimination and/or group prejudice. (b) Amazingly but fittingly, male Chinese students exhibited less social distance toward other national and ethnic groups than did female, which would account for the gender differential in exogamy among the Chinese.

In another study conducted by Sinha and Upadhyay, 100 male and 100 female subjects were tested for their attitudes toward nine different ethnic groups: Americans, Chinese, English, French, Germans, Indians, Negroes, Pakistanis, and Russians (43). There was a gender differential in the desirability assigned to the various groups. Males assigned maximum desirable characteristics to light-skinned groups. Female students not only gave maximum desir-

able characteristics to light-skinned groups, but assigned a minimum to the dark-skinned. Such persons have migrated to America
in significant numbers since coming to help build the California
railroads. The attitudes they carried about dark-skinned people
both facilitate the colonization of and enable the subjugation of
oppressed populations. With few exceptions, they understand that
racism is a daily part of life in the U.S. At every turn and in every
situation racism manages to remind Asian-Americans that they are
less than others. It cuts to their self worth and human dignity
despite the obvious prohibitions against discrimination and racism, the rights to asylum, right to information, protection of the
family, and a cultural identity (44). This reality, more than anything else, motivated their dark-skinned African-American counterpart to assert themselves and fight for human rights in every
possible forum and in every possible way at their disposal.

Perhaps most indicative of racism is the fact that although
Asian-Americans make significant contributions to two cultures
economically, politically, socially, etc. like chattel they themselves
remain on the fringes and are otherwise dependent. Their lives are
contingent upon their subjugation to the Euro-American mainstream. In a post-colonial era, fulfilling their own needs is secondary to contending with subjugation. There is little doubt that if
such people were given equality they could not be oppressed with
immunity. However, the impositions of colonization continue to
compromise their efforts, leaving them to manage little more from
life than a struggle from day to day.

The ability of America to maintain post-colonial domination
depends principally upon its somatic visibility and its acceptance
of Western superiority as skin color ideal. However, the mere belief
in superiority is not enough to sustain the phenomenon. Mechanisms must be constructed to denigrate and reinforce a human
hierarchy by differentiation. Included are: (a) the use of stereotypes, which leads to subjugation; (b) the use of legal barriers and
norms, which leads to a competitive disadvantage; and (c) differentiation by stigmatization of subjugated populations (45). Thus,

how a post-colonial Asian-American group is treated is a function of its perceived threat, its unpopularity, and the enforcement power of the colonizing entity. Frequently, the eruption of a crisis rationalizes extreme actions that may even include extermination. Prevalent in the aftermath, are exiles, refugees, and genocide. The more excessive actions tend to occur when prejudice, discrimination, and segregation have exacted their toll.

Migrant Asians who settle in America and marry exogamously exhibit a color-based hierarchy commensurate with Euro-American somatic ideals. In America, where race dominates skin color is strictly applied to social and political group interaction. Whereas Euro-Americans may be differentiated by socially selected cultural traits, in America Asian-Americans—as people of color—are distinguished by socially selected physical traits, i.e. alien skin (46). Designation by cultural group traits would have little or no meaning if the dominant group neither recognized nor acknowledged such traits as stigmata. Hence, in America, the classification of Asians as alien is dependent on the perceptions and definitions held by members of the post-colonial mainstream. Whereas some Euro-Americans do not fit the American ideal, they are not differentiated as alien to its skin color norm. They do not regard themselves as stigmatized nor are they so regarded by the mainstream population (47). It is only when social and cultural attributes are associated with distinct physical features in a way that denigrates that the concept of ideal takes on special significance (48). Subsequently, Asians in America suffer forms of racism extended from their being perceived as alien; these are perpetrated not only by the civil segments of the dominant group but also by dark-skinned members of subjugated populations as well—a manifestation of racism (49). Thus, Asian-Americans, by comparison, encounter assimilation experiences quite distinct from Euro-American groups who may not conform to the ideal. Their inability to conform accordingly for racist reasons in a post-colonial era has visited murder upon otherwise innocent Asian-American citizens.

On a warm summer day in June of 1982, a 27 year-old Chinese-American named Vincent Chin proceeded to a Detroit bar with three friends (50). He had gone there to celebrate the occasion of his upcoming marriage. Unknown to him and his friends, at the time there were two Euro-American auto-workers attending the same bar. The older was named Ronald Ebens, who was accompanied by his step-son, Michael Nitz. When Chin and his friends encountered the two Ebens and his step-son began hurling racial slurs at Chin, reportedly incorrectly calling him, a "Jap." Ebens shouted: "It's because of you, mother f—, that we're out of work!" Shortly after his comment, fighting began. In an effort to restore calm, the manager ejected both groups. After they left the bar, Ebens and Nitz proceeded to their car. One of the two then opened the trunk of the car and removed a baseball bat. There is some dispute as to the following events, but they then went after Chin and his friends who were waiting in the bar's parking lot to be picked up by a friend. Once Ebens and Nitz were in sight, Chin and his friends, attempted to escape. Ebens and his step-son pursued them until they caught Chin. They caught him alone in front of a McDonald's restaurant. The step-son proceeded to restrain Chin while Ebens began beating him about the head with the wooden baseball bat. Eventually Chin lost consciousness from the brutality and was reported to have said to a friend just prior: "It isn't fair." Not long after, Chin died as a result of massive head wounds sustained from the beating. What had started out as a celebration of his impending wedding ended with his funeral.

The murder of Vincent Chin pointedly illustrates the existence of racism beyond the black/white dichotomy. Chin's assailants had drawn upon the hushed reality of racism in America to vent their rage against anyone who looked Asian. They were very typical Euro-American auto workers in their socio-economic backgrounds, but must have felt entitled by racial rights to exploit Asian-American lives as they saw fit. They were not criminals in the traditional sense, which makes their crime even more horrendous. Until he was laid off, Ebens had worked as a foreman at one of the local automobile plants in the Detroit area. Nitz had been laid off as well, but was attending school part-time. Eventually Ebens and Nitz were charged with second-degree murder. In a post-colonial era, where then president Richard Nixon had raved about getting "tough" on crime, Ebens and his step-son were given the opportunity to plead guilty to a lesser charge of manslaughter. The presiding judge in their case—Charles S. Kaufman—handed down his decision on March 16, 1983. Based upon arguments from the defense attorneys and without hearing from the prosecuting attorney, Kaufman freed both men on probation and fined them $3000.00 plus court fees for the murder of an innocent Asian-American. Ebens and Nitz had taunted Chin for his color in the same way Ying Ma had done to African-Americans, but no African-American has ever murdered an Asian-American in a fit of racial rage. This otherwise significant fact is irrelevant to some because it is not conducive to their perspective. Conversely, much of the nation was outraged by this seeming miscarriage of justice. Kaufman defended his judgement by defending the assailants. He agreed to allow them to pay $125 a month for what they had done. He insisted that Ebens and Nitz "weren't the kind of men you send to jail." "We're talking here about a man (Ebens) who's held down a responsible job with the same company for seventeen or eighteen years and his son (Nitz) who is employed and is a part-time student. . . . These men are not going to go out and harm somebody else." The usual mantras of justice, law, and order were conspicuously silenced. Kaufman curiously did not feel it necessary to put the culprits in jail, stating: "putting them in prison wouldn't do any good for them or for society. . . . You don't make the punishment fit the crime; you make the punishment fit the criminal."

No doubt, Chin's family was outraged. His mother in particular took issue with an American system of justice where there were no consequences for those who would take an Asian life. Although Chin's mother was an immigrant, she had learned quickly the workings of American jurist prudence. In a fit of anger she asked: "What kind of law is this? What kind of justice?" "This happened because my son is Chinese. If two Chinese killed a white person, they must go to jail, maybe for their whole lives . . . Something is wrong with this country." But Ms. Chin's words found little support from a post-colonial style criminal justice system.

As expected, news of Vincent Chin's murder galvanized the Asian-American community, which was outraged by Judge Kaufman's decision and the light sentences he imposed upon the murderers. In Detroit, the Asian-American community organized the American Citizens for Justice and demanded a review of the light sentences. They contacted the United States Department of Justice to demand an investigation of the case as having violated Chin's federal civil rights. According to this organization, Judge Kaufman had in effect given Ebens and Nitz a license to kill Asian-Americans for $3,000.

Members of Congress also pitched in to request an investigation of the judge and the Wayne County officials who were involved. In fact, evidence was found that Chin's rights had been violated, which resulted in a federal grand jury being convened in September of 1983. A short time later, Ebens and Nitz were indicted on two counts. A year later, Ebens was convicted in federal court of violating Chin's civil rights. Nitz was acquitted on all charges. It appeared that some semblance of justice had prevailed as Ebens was sentenced to 25 years in jail and treatment for alcoholism. He maintained his freedom after posting $20,000 in bond.

Following his conviction Ebens hired an attorney to appeal his case, which was overturned in September of 1986 on a legal technicality. In response, the Justice Department then scheduled a retrial, which moved the case from the Detroit community, where the crime had occurred, to Cincinnati. As could have been expected, a Cincinnati jury found Ebens innocent of all charges brought by the Justice Department. This decision terminated the case of Vincent Chin. In the era of Nixon's "get tough on crime" two Euro-Americans—unlike African-Americans—had brutally murdered an innocent Asian-American with minimum legal consequence. Chin's mother, Lily Chin, was so upset by the verdict that she returned out of disgust to her native Chinese homeland. As per the murder of Vincent Chin, racism in the post-colonial era implies the ability of Euro-Americans to impose their perspectives as psychic ideals in the absence of consideration of Asian-American reaction (51). Regardless of the particular methods used, Euro-Americans may then construct an Asian-American psyche extended from Euro-American prescriptions not irrelevant to skin color. Furthermore, aside from the more obvious tactics, psychological colonization may encourage Asian-American racism by skin color as in the case of Ying Ma. In the West, Euro-Americans have always been in a position to impose their ideals upon Asian-Americans who have been stigmatized as alien to their skin color norm (52). As individuals, Euro-Americans may act out domination of Asian-Americans in particular without ever making conscious or overt decisions to do so. The willingness of Asian-American women, in particular, to acquiesce is rooted in their having been socialized to pursue the "American Dream" via the Euro-American male. As pertains to the dynamics of this scenario, research suggests dominant groups accordingly acquire power directly by emphasizing competence and action. Colonized groups acquire power by virtue of identification with and/or subjugation to dominant group ideals, i.e.: the marriage of conservative Senator Phil Gramm to Asian-American Wendy Lee Gramm (53). Given the status differential, resulting interactions between Asian-Americans and dominant group Euro-Americans are thus tantamount to institutionalized racism. The Asian-American concept of beauty is not irrelevant to that racism.

In the post-colonial era, Asian-American skin color and other physical attributes are frequently denigrated by Asian-Americans themselves. In referring to such attributes, Hoetink uses the concept of "somatic norm image" (54). By definition it is "the complex of physical somatic characteristics accepted as ideal" (55). Hence, every healthy group psyche considers itself aesthetically superior to all others. But as pertains to racism, an American somatic norm implies the belief that superiority is physiologically based in the Euro-American racial category. Any deviations from said category are presumed inferior, enabling various social and political objectives. Accordingly, the psychological implications of racism for Asian-Americans are as follows: (a) somatic ideals are continually rooted in Euro-American ideals, although it is seldom articulated in polite circles; (b) by virtue of colonization such ideals are inculcated by Asian-Americans as the norm and a prerequisite to assimilation; (c) the effort of Asian-Americans to then migrate to America has necessitated manifestation of a skin color hierarchy; (d) in its aftermath prevails a less Asian and more Euro-American light/white skin as the preferred somatic Asian-American ideal.

Thus, racism and skin color among people of color is no longer a question of existence but rather the extent of its impediment. Both America and its Asian citizens are impacted by racism, requiring a more comprehensive understanding of its dynamics. A focus upon skin color will enable social scientists to confront and devise an appropriate course of action for presenting problems. Although there are people of all races who make earnest attempts to eliminate racism, their numbers are few. They struggle daily against racist agendas because the success of their efforts would result in a dramatic shift in wealth and power. Immediate eradication of racism would liberate oppressed and vulnerable populations at expense of the dominant group power structure, which McIntosh refers to as "white privilege" (56). Accordingly, their lifestyle would be significantly altered and more commensurate with social justice.

Given the existent Western power differential, Asian-Americans initially directed their liberation efforts at European ethnic groups. Eventually their circuitous experience with racism enabled their own racism and/or personal victimization. Racism in America remains a dominant force. However, by definition, it is no longer—and perhaps never was—perpetuated solely by those of European descent. The rhetoric of social justice has necessitated the incorporation of Asian-Americans and other people of color into the fold of perpetrators in order to remain potent and viable. In the aftermath of colonization, imperialism, and various forms of European domination racism by skin color prevails. As an alternative to the traditional view of racism being solely a "black vs. white" concept, focus on skin color is put forth as a workable starting point for ending all forms of oppression by better understanding the dynamics of human interaction more globally. Hence from a less biased perspective, the existence of racism and its association with skin color is not contingent upon whether or not accusations meet the standards of law, but that racism is a universal dynamic of the human environment. No other aspect of racism has been as insulated from scholarly debate and publication as manifestations among people of color. It is reflected among Asian-Americans and similar to a variation of "white" racism (57). It is apparent in Ghandi's apathy to the murder of black Africans in his South African struggle (58). These horrendous events enabled the metastasizing of racism to the world's human social environment. Infecting Asian-Americans is the eventual end-result.

Enabled by Asian-American naïveté, the role of racists in their perpetuation of racism is now more insidious than ever but less conspicuous. It is detectable in the omission of skin color issues from human behavior texts by social work scholars (59). It is detectable in institutions of higher education that include social justice in their mission statements yet make no official effort to export diversity abroad to countries known to actively discriminate against dark-skinned people. Hence, upon entering a new millennium, America and other Western nations must be the geopolitical starting point of social justice and efforts to rescue humanity from the perils of racism in the post-colonial era. Europe, Australia, Canada, the United States and other post-colonials are obligated to a higher standard of activism and moral excellence. Their ability to rescue humanity, as well as themselves, can be accomplished by focusing their energies upon the elimination of skin color as a vehicle of racism. As the mainstay of oppression, this elimination will render all forms of oppression moot and enable the worldwide viability of equality and social justice.

References

(1) New York Times. (5/9/00). San Francisco outlaws size bias. Times Fax, p. 3.

(2)   Solomon, A. (1992). Clinical diagnosis among diverse populations: a multicultural perspective. Families in Society: The Journal of Contemporary Human Services, 73(6), 371-377.

(3) OECD (1999). World Development Indicators. Washington, D.C.

(4) Cohen, R. (June 23, 2000). Britain Charges Truck Driver in 58 Deaths. New York: Times Fax, p. 2.

(5) Hernton, C. (1965). Sex and Racism in America. New York: Grove.

(6) Stember, C. (1976). Sexual Racism. New York: Elsevier Scientific.

(7) Steiner, L. (1987). Case work as a private venture. Journal of Independent Social Work, 2(1), 57-70.

(8) Longres, J. & Seltzer, G. (1994). Racism: its implications for the education of minority social work students. Journal of Multicultural Social Work, 3(1), 59-75.

(9) Banerjee, S. (1985). Assortive mating for color in Indian population. Journal of Biosocial Science, 17, 205-209.

(10) Hall, R. E. (October, 1992). Bias among African-Americans regarding skin color: Implications for social work practice. Research on Social Work Practice, 2(4), 479-486.

(11) Schiele, J. (1994). Afrocentricity as an alternative world view for equality. Journal of Progressive Human Services, 5(1), 5-25.

(12) Kitano, H. (1985). Race relations. Englewood Cliffs, NJ: Prentice-Hall.

(13) Hall, R. E. (1990). The projected manifestations of aspiration, personal values, and environmental assessment cognates of cutaneo-chroma (skin color) for a selected population of African Americans (Doctoral dissertation, Atlanta University, 1989). Dissertation Abstracts International, 50, 3363A.

(14) Vontress, C. (1970). Counseling Black. Personnel and Guidance Journal, 48, 713-719.

(15) Farhard, D. (1988). Jung: A racist. British Journal of Psychotherapy, 4, pp. 263-279.

(16) Morrow vs the Internal Revenue Service, 742 F. Supp. 670 (N.D. Ga. 1990).

(17) Rabinowitz, H. (1978). Race relations in the urban south. New York: Oxford University Press.

(18) Anderson, L. (1991). Acculturative stress: A theory of relevance to Black Americans. Clinical Psychology Review. 11(6). 685-702.

(19) Reuter, E. (1969). The mulatto in the United States. New York: Haskell House.

(20) Banerjee, S. (1985). Assortive mating for color in Indian population. Journal of Biosocial Science, 17, 205-209.

(21) Washington, R. (1990). Brown Racism and the Formation of a World System of Racial Stratification. International Journal of Politics, Culture, and Society, 4(2), 209-227.

(22) Washington, R. (1990). Brown Racism and the Formation of a World System of Racial Stratification. International Journal of Politics, Culture, and Society, 4(2), 209-227.

(23) Kim, K. (1990). Blacks Against Korean Merchants: An Interpretation of Contributory Factors. Migration World Magazine, 18(5), 11-15.

(24) Harvey, A. (1995). The issue of skin color in psychotherapy with African Americans. Families in Society, 76 (1),

(25) Banerjee, S. (1985). Assortive mating for color in Indian population. Journal of Biosocial Science, 17, 205-209.

(26) Shinagawa, L. & Pang, G. (1988). Intraethnic, and interra-

cial marriages among Asian-Americans in California, 1980. Berkeley Journal of Sociology, 33, 95-114.

(27) Hall, R. (1996). Eurogamy among Asian-Americans: implications of skin color for assimilation. Manuscript submitted for publication.

(28) Hall, R. E. (1994). The "bleaching syndrome": Implications of light skin for Hispanic American assimilation. Hispanic Journal of Behavioral Sciences, 16(3), 307-314.

(29) Haslam, N. (1995). Factor Structure of Social Relationships: An Examination of Relational Models and Resource Exchange Theories. Journal of Social and Personal Relationships, 12(2), 217-227.

(30) Akio, Y. & Mace, F. (1995). Avoiding Impurity: Civilization Processes in Ancient Japan. Annales, 50(2), 283-306.

(31) Das, M. (1976). A Cross National Study of Intercaste Conflict in India and the U.S. International Journal of Contemporary Sociology, 13(3-4), 261-277.

(32) Kikumura, A. & Kitano, H. (1973). Interracial Marriage: A Picture of the Japanese Americans. Journal of Social Issues, 29(2), 67-81.

(33) Washington, R. (1990). Brown Racism and the Formation of a World System of Racial Stratification. International Journal of Politics, Culture, and Society, 4(2), 209-227.

(34) Ibid

(35) Mannoni, O. (1956). Prospero and Caliban: the psychology of colonization. New York: Praeger.

(36) Garrett, K. (1999). Are Asians Racist? http://www.abc.net.au/rn/talks/bbing/stories/s36894. html.

(37) Chang, I. (1997). The Rape of Nanking. New York: Penguin Books.

(38) Ibid

(39) Garrett, K. (1999). Are Asians Racist? http://www.abc.net.au/rn/talks/bbing/stories/s36894. html.

(40) Washington, R. (1990). Brown Racism and the Formation of

a World System of Racial Stratification. International Journal of Politics, Culture, and Society, 4(2), 209-227.

(41) Garrett, K. (1999). Are Asians Racist? http://www.abc.net.au/rn/talks/bbing/stories/s36894.html.

(42) Kuo-Shu, Y., Pen-Hua, L. & Ching-Fang, Y. (1963). The social distance attitudes of Chinese students towards 25 national and ethnic groups. Acta Psychologica Taiwanica, 5, 37-51.

(43) Sinha, A. & Upadhyay, O. (1960). Stereotypes of male and female university students in India towards the different ethnic groups. Journal of Social Psychology, 51, 93-102.

(44) Kitano, H. (1997). Race Relations. Englewood Cliffs, NJ: Prentice-Hall.

(45) Banerjee, S. (1985). Assortive mating for color in Indian populations. The Journal of Bioscience, 17, pp. 205-209.

(46) Hyde, C. (1995). The meanings of whiteness. Qualitative Sociology, 18(1), pp. 87-95.

(47) Cooley, C. (1902). Human Nature and the Social Order. Schreiber, N.Y.

(48) Phinney, J. & Alipuria, L. (1996). At the interface of cultures: multiethnic/multiracial high school and college students. The Journal of Social Psychology, 136, 139-158.

(49) Wonderly, D. (1996). The selfish gene pool: An evolutionary stable system. University Press of America, Ohio.

(50) Takaki, R. Who killed Vincent Chin? In A look beyond the model minority image (Ed.). Grace Yun.

(51) Chan, S. (1991). Asian Americans: an interpretive history. Boston: Twayne.

(52) Hedley, M. (1994). The presentation of gendered conflict in popular movies: Affective stereotypes, cultural sentiments, and men's motivation. Sex Rles, 31, 721-740.

(53) Hoetink, H. (1967). The two variants in Caribbean race relations: A contribution to the sociology of segmented societies. Trans. E. M. Hookykaas, New York, N.Y.

(54) Snowden, F. (1991). Before color prejudice. Harvard University Press. Cambridge, M.A.

(55) Sahay, S. (1994). Satisfaction among South Asian Canadien and European Canadien female university students. (Ethnic Identificaton). ProQuest File: Dissertation Abstracts, Item: 13.

(56) McIntosh, P. (1989). White Privilege: Unpacking the invisible napsack. Peace and Freedom, July/August, 10-12.

(57) Hall, R. E. (1997). Eurogamy Among Asian Americans: A Note on Western Assimilation. Social Science Journal 34(3), pp. 403-408.

(58) Washington, R. (1990). Brown Racism and the Formation of a World System of Racial Stratification. International Journal of Politics, Culture, and Society, 4(2), 209-227.

(59) Zastrow, C. & Kirst-Ashman, K. (1990). Understanding Human Behavior in the Social Environment. Chicago: Nelson-Hall Pub.

IV

Post-Colonial Bias

According to Loeb, colonial bias is little more than a manifestation of profanity (1). Biases in general are determined on the basis of some observed phenomenon within the environment of human perception. Skin color bias is a manifestation of post-colonization and results from generalizations based on the negative interpretations of phenotypical characteristics, which in the case of Asian-Americans is critical to disrupting their mental health and reducing quality of life. Bias on the basis of skin color is a reoccurring pattern that evolved from the generalizations of Western culture. Indicative of colonization, as persons are acknowledged by the color of their skin they are assigned labels to denote differentiation, how they behave, and some predetermined status value. Once such persons have been effectively codified the tendency is to dismiss their individuality as pertains to character or accomplishment thereby enabling the cycle of bias (2).

Among migrant Asians, skin color and socioeconomic status are bias criteria for assessing potential. More often Asians characterized by Western-like phenotype or financial stability will be better suited to assimilate into their Western host country. The dark skin of other Asians remains in contrast to their Western counterparts. With the exception of the middle and upper classes—who have no need to migrate—most are poor. Their reasons for leaving their mother country include the search for a better life. Unfortunately, life in their host countries offers a new set of social problems they may not have encountered in their native land. Such problems as racial discrimination, poor working conditions, and service standards selectively applied by Western venders, seem to be associated with the darker-skinned Asians' conspicuous and/ or exotic phenotype. Such prejudicial treatment is a norm of Western culture that has no doubt psychologically affected Asian-Americans. Their lack of power enabled the evolution of restrictions that were placed on members of their community—both male and female. This prejudicial process with some limitation absorbed most migrants into the mainstream of Western society, with one exception: Africans and those with similarly dark skin and exotic features. After decades of denigration, dark-skinned Asians in particular have migrated to America despite obstacles to their acceptance. This study, rather than focussing upon the biases of Americans, attempts to determine whether the biases that Asian-Americans have been subjected to, both historically and in the present, have been internalized. The objectivity of that attempt is best served by comparison with a similarly colonized population of Hispanics.

Travel brochures to Hispanic nations aptly profess the rich variation in skin color and other phenotypes among people. Vacationing tourists are impressed by the seeming lack of bias that residents proudly attest to. Unmentionable, however, is the bias against Hispanics, characterized by dark skin. The existence of such prejudice is invisible to the casual observer but is immune to dispute in the aftermath of colonization.

Bias, on some basis, is as old as America itself. However, its manifestation among Hispanics on the basis of skin color is all but oblivious to the casual observer. Furthermore, among Hispanics, current forms of bias are the direct result of having been militarily colonized by Westerners from Spain and socially colonized by Westerners from the U.S. mainland (3). Following their various acts of domination vis-á-vis the island's cultural mores, Spanish colonials evolved a status hierarchy to discourage any notions of merit attributable to non-Western and/or dark-skinned populations (4). The uppermost in status among Hispanics became those whose heritage most approximates that of the light-skinned colonists and the least being an opposite extreme (5). In an effort to comply, Hispanics had been imposed upon by a homogeneous racial system that is in many ways not only alien but psychologically debilitating. For such a heterogeneous population, the effort to maintain doctrines of racial purity did not evolve with the same vigor as was characteristic of the U.S. mainland. While color bias is not totally irrelevant as a social phenomenon to Hispanics, by U.S. standards it is much less potent. In the absence of a virulent race tradition, bias has prevailed in a more stealthy and subtle form.

Color bias among Hispanics exists because it is ubiquitous among Spanish colonies. The longevity of its manifestation preceded American influence. The ignorance applicable to skin color bias is not surprising since the issue is frequently regarded as "taboo" (6). Among Hispanics the myth of racial indifference helps preserve "personalismo" (warmth, openess, and personal attentiveness). As a consequence, aside from a subtle but tenacious idealization of light skin there is more celebration in social life and courtship among Hispanics than among Americans. Despite that fact, research conducted as far back as 1949 suggested that, although some Hispanics denied the existence of bias, 50% felt it was better to have light skin regardless of racial heritage (7). No one felt it was better to be dark. The custom of entertaining dark-skinned relatives in the kitchen, much like servants, is a common notion and not unknown to Hispanics who migrate to the U.S. mainland. Such a notion implied that among relatives some are less preferred than others, precipitating family disjointure (8).

The existence of bias among Hispanics is dramatically validated by litigation. One of the first cases of skin color bias and/or discrimination brought by Hispanic-Americans was in 1981, that of the dark-skinned Felix—plaintiff—versus the lighter-skinned Marquez—defendant, decided by the U.S. District Court of the District of Columbia. The plaintiff alleges that the defendant did not promote her on the basis of skin color bias. At trial, the plain-

tiff introduced the personnel cards of twenty-eight of her former
fellow employees. She testified that, among them, only two were
as dark or darker in color than she. All of the other employees in
the office, according to the plaintiff, were light-skinned. Other
highly credible evidence presented to the court suggested, however, that she might have been in error.

As per defendant, the plaintiff was not entitled to a promotion
in grade by virtue of her position, her qualifications, her seniority,
and/or her length of service. The evidence showed that her employer awarded promotions in grade based upon criteria that were
neutral with respect to skin color. Employees whose color was as
dark or darker than the plaintiff's were given promotions in grade,
while many other employees who were lighter than she were given
infrequent promotions, or no promotions at all. Similar neutrality
with respect to skin color was evident in the promotions in grade
among employees throughout the entire agency. Based upon the
rules of legal proceeding, the accused did not discriminate against
the plaintiff based on her color in failing to recommend her for a
promotion in grade. Thus, the court decided that the plaintiff was
not promoted in grade for legitimate business reasons having nothing whatsoever to do with her skin color (9).

A more recent case, Felero versus Stryker, was litigated in 1998.
Falero, the plaintiff is a dark-skinned male while Rigoberto, the
corporation defendant, is a light-skinned male. The plaintiff claims
he was terminated from his job on the basis of having dark skin.
The defendant contends that the plaintiff did not establish that
he was replaced by someone not within the protected class. The
defendant further stated that the plaintiff's job had not been filled
by anyone, but admits one of his areas of work was assigned to
another employee. Thus, direct evidence of skin color discrimination was lacking.

A loss in litigation should not suggest color bias does not exist
among Hispanic-Americans. Indeed, the accusation makes apparent existence of the issue. While the evidence in the aforementioned cases does not rise to the level of legal guilt, it fits a pattern

of bias little acknowledged in the scholarly literature; that bias is not peculiar to Hispanic-Americans, but is instead an unmentionable dynamic associated with the social milieu of post-colonial territories.

Other evidence has verified that Hispanic-Americans are quite sensitive in reference to skin color. Some, adamantly, avoid identification with darker-skinned people of color. Data collected from Hispanic- and Euro-American subjects in recent decades have verified high rejection rates toward all descendants of Africans. This is essentially true among those living in rural areas, as shown on the table below. As expected, intermarriage evoked the highest resistance. Attitude studies of Hispanic-Americans in Bakersfield, Los Angeles, and San Antonio further confirm these findings, with all groups overwhelmingly opposing intermarriage with African-Americans as per dark skin color (10).

Rejection rates of African-Americans via levels of encounter

	White	Spanish-Speak	Urban Mex	Rural Mex
By marriage	89.4	62.8	59.0	78.4
As neighbors	50.7	45.4	43.2	71.5
As co-work	21.1	8.0	39.2	70.0
For citizenshp	5.1	4.3	41.5	74.9

Loomis, 1970

There are marked differences between older and younger Mexican-Americans regarding dark skin and its relevance to identity. The older members who struggled for their citizenship gave less priority to skin color than did youth. Until recently, it was common for Mexican-Americans to trace their ancestry by way of their Hispano genes (11). This need to identify with the "superior" Anglo group has caused some to ascribe "whiteness" to the Aztec nation. Once a dark-skinned person has internalized the idea that light skin is more desirable, he begins to develop a negative attitude toward self. An intense self-hatred then produces feelings of inferiority. This acceptance of dark skin as a sign of inferiority begins earlier than grade school (12). Experiments show that ascribing badness to dark colors and goodness to whites, seeing dark objects as smaller than they actually are and seeing white objects as larger, and other positive/negative color evaluations begin in early childhood. Having darker skin color self-hate results with adverse effects on the victim's personal motivation. When opportunities are consistently offered to the lighter-skinned Hispanic-Americans in the larger society, despair develops among the darker-skinned. This is witnessed by Hispanic-American youth in Castroville, California:

> "The teenage boys said there wasn't much use of finishing High School if you are dark . . . you couldn't get a good job anyway … girls who recently graduated from High School reported that they had many difficulties in finding secretarial or clerical jobs in the Castroville and Salinas area. They said that girls who looked almost white got jobs first but that some of the . . . girls never did find the kind of employment they sought and finally had to go to work in the sheds of the local packing company" (13).

Skin color consciousness among Hispanic-Americans disrupts group cohesion and sets up marital barriers. Adult parents wonder whether children of "mixed" marriages will be rejected by the dark-skinned parent or be accepted by the light-skinned parent. Some Hispanic-American girls admitted that they spurned Euro-American boyfriends for fear they would have to choose between identifying with a dark-skinned offspring and maintaining acceptance by their light-skinned spouse, an issue no less relevant to Asian-Americans (14).

Asian, as it refers to the people, is a broad term. It connotes the various ethnic groups that comprise the Mongoloid race. While Asians are Mongoloids who can be very different culturally, "racially" they are brought together by their gene pool. Furthermore, within each Asian ethnic group exists beliefs and practices common and unique for each of the separate groupings. One characteristic, however, that does seem to be indicative of a large number of both American and other Asian ethnic groups, is their tendency to marry within the group. In countries, such as Canada, Great Britain, and Australia, the phenomenon is widespread. Additionally, in some Asian cultures such as Japan, the concept of attractiveness had been associated with light skin long before they ever had contact with the West. It is reflected in their almost 50% rate of Euro "marrying out" in America during the 1970s (15). Thus, for Japanese who began to migrate to America in large numbers where light skin was already the norm, marrying out was helped along by what had seemed culturally preferred.

In the analysis of Asian-Americans, no one is more esteemed than Dr. Harry L. Kitano. Dr. Kitano is not well known for his work that has provided insight into the study of Asian-Americans. According to Dr. Kitano, Asian assimilation takes place in America by way of a process he calls the "domination model." His book, entitled: *Race Relations* explains the concept. Simply put, the "domination model" would mean that assimilation is a dictated process whereby a powerful group—in this case Euro-Americans—withholds or bestows societal reward on the basis of what it values in its people. In a society that turns on the wheels of competition, assimilation for those who are not valued can be a painful process. And for those who cannot or will not, compete, for whatever reasons, opportunity and quality of life will be negatively impacted. Thus, given that Euro light skin is highly valued in America's people, Asian-Americans are at a disadvantage in most matters of competition with Euro-Americans. They cannot compete, at least to an equal extent because they lack the necessary criteria for assimilation. And, unfortunately, they do not have a choice in the matter because alien skin color and eye shape are not subject to the will of those so characterized. Yet, historically embracing Euro-American culture has been a tradition for the successful assimilation or acceptance of groups into the mainstream of American society. That is, any group wishing to become American must not only embrace but fit the criteria, as defined, of what is an American. That pertains to Asians, Hispanics, and Euro-Americans, other than the WASP ideal.

Without hesitation, Asians who left their homeland and ventured to American shores were eager for acceptance and gave little consideration to the prospect of what assimilation might require of them. More than anything, they sought the opportunity to become citizens of undoubtedly the richest and most powerful nation the world has ever known. Certainly, each in their various ways paid a price in discrimination including non-WASP Euro-Americans. Every religious, racial, or culturally distinct faction of what has come to be regarded as the "American patchwork" experienced it. But for members of Euro ethnic groups, being physically similar to the mainstream, assimilation was of less concern. That is, while "white" ethnic groups experienced discrimination, their gene pool already satisfied the criteria for acceptance. For immigrants of Asian descent, assimilation was obviously not as workable as it was for Euro-Americans. Furthermore, those who became acculturated and accepted the religious persuasion of the dominant population continued to encounter challenges to their authenticity as Americans. The physical features indicative of belonging to their gene pool were reinforced by the cultural tradition of most Asian ethnics. The tendency of Asian males to marry within their group made Asian-Americans appear even more alien than what might otherwise have been. After several generations, unlike Euro immigrants, Asians remained physically conspicuous on the patchwork of America's ethnic landscape. Their most distinct "yellow skin" and "slanted" eyes marked them as exotics in a land where their families may have lived for a hundred years or more! In the throes of acculturation and a desire to be accepted as the "card-carrying" Americans they already were, Asian-Americans, not necessarily with intent, then set about altering their physical features in order to join the gene pool of Euro-America.

Commensurate with the domination model, Asian-Americans are regarded as "minorities." The most potent aspect of their identity as "minorities" is their particular skin color. The issue of skin color among them has remained a significant part of Asian culture for quite some time. That is true whether or not they migrated. In Great Britain, it was enabled by British colonization, and, as a result, Asians internalized light skin as a norm because they were powerless under colonization to contest the influence of the dominant colonizing population. But unlike that population internalization of light skin as an ideal resulted in psychic conflict, because skin color is immediately and undeniably verifiable upon sight. It is not only applied by Euro ethnics in America to assess the assimilation potential of groups, but by Asian-Americans in general to assess the assimilation potential of individual members. For them it is reflected in how they perceive attractiveness, who they decide to marry, and in other life choices where skin color may be subjectively applied. The entire process is not necessarily a malicious act although it may be. They may not only be biased against people of color but Euro-Americans as well.

In many Asian languages the words "fair" and "beautiful" are often used synonymously (16). Asian folk literature places a high value on light skin. For example, the ideal bride, whose beauty and virtue are praised in the songs sung at weddings, almost always has a light complexion. An Asian girl who is dark-skinned is often a problem for her family because of the difficulty of arranging a marriage for her. Marriages among educated Asians are sometimes arranged through advertisements in the newspapers; even a casual examination of the matrimonial columns shows that virginity and a light skin color are among the most desirable qualities that men and their families look for in a young bride, especially the middle class. In a society where purity of descent is associated with a wide diversity of physical types, these features may be in short supply. Those who do not correspond to the ideal must be accommodated. Among some Asians, then, a dark-skinned girl has a low value in the marriage market. But, at the same time, a dark-skinned girl may be preferred by her local group. Wherever physical differences cut across caste lines—and they frequently do—the factor of culture can carry greater weight. That is sure to confuse outsiders. And while there is clearly a preference for light skin in almost all sections of Asian society, it is difficult to define the social implications. The best evidence is to be found in the choice of marriage partners. The choice of a light-skinned bride or groom must be made, however, within limits that are strictly defined by considerations of other kinds, such as culture, group, locale, etc. Thus, in certain parts of Asia women are very light-skinned and have features that are positively valued. However, this does not seem to negate the fact that a bride, be she light-skinned, would not normally be acceptable in any household. Ultimately, skin color of a particular kind is somewhat important to Asians, but other characteristics are not irrelevant.

Light skin has much greater weight in choosing an Asian bride than an Asian groom. In the case of the groom, qualities such as wealth, occupation, and education play an important role. Skin color is important but secondary. To marry off a dark-skinned son is not so much of a problem in either case for a middle class family, for he can more easily acquire other socially desirable traits unlike color which is set at birth. For Asian grooms, the norms for attractiveness relative to light skin in America and in the "old country" are no less important than they are for women—but for different reasons. In general, those who have light skin may be regarded as more strikingly handsome (17). But that belief alone does not necessarily determine their overall appeal because it may not coincide with group norms for masculinity or sex appeal. However, consistent with the greater attractiveness value placed upon light skin, Asian men with darker skin are viewed as more sinister and threatening by both the upper and lower caste populations. One such example are the scores of dark-skinned, male, Asian stars in film who play the role of villain while their lighter-skinned counterparts play the role of leading man or hero (18).

Asian-American females, like many dark-skinned African-Americans, may then be saddened by their appearance. Society, unfortunately, demands physical beauty in females much more so than males. Since the degree of assimilation closely correlates with the way one looks, light skin has emerged as an ideal among both male and female Asians because they are Americans who obviously do not have it and require it to feel acceptable. Thus, the skin color issue among Asian-Americans is germane to American culture and its obsession with light skin. It was brought about by the importation/migration of Asians that began when they were brought over to work on the railroads in large numbers. Having a long history in America, Asian ethnics have idealized light skin because they were powerless to contest the influence of the dominant population. But, unlike that population, the idealization has resulted in conflict because their contrast in skin color is immediately and undeniably verifiable upon sight. For Asians, it is different from the experience of a Jew, an Italian, or any other Euro ethnic. They cannot hide. They should not want to or have to. Furthermore, they have few options where their features are concerned. Thus, the skin color and eye shape issue for Asian-Americans has undoubtedly become very important. It is not merely applied by Euro-Americans—however subconsciously—to assess the assimilation potential of other groups, but by Asian-Americans to assess the assimilation potential of one another as well. Sung, a scholar of Asian-American studies, inferred this notion by way of research contained in one of her books, entitled *Interracial Marriage Among Chinese-Americans*.

The high rate of marrying out, her book suggests, should come as no surprise. It is reflected in the disproportionate number of Chinese "out marriages" to Euro-Americans compiled by the U.S. Census Bureau. The issue is light skin. Knowing that, it should then be plausible to assume that interracial marriage among Asian-Americans would occur mostly with Euro-Americans because they are the ideal and least with African-Americans because they are dark-skinned. If part of the reasoning for this is attributed to the greater number of Euro-Americans, cultural notions about people with dark skin cannot be ignored. The entire process of interracial marriage, although it can be, is not necessarily a malicious act. Asian-Americans are not racist, as might be said of some Euro-

Americans. They are like all people of color who carry the label "minority"—simply colonized.

For generations, Asian-Americans have lived and died upon American soil and assimilated to some extent. They have done so despite segregation and social isolation. They have experienced American wars and American social changes. Like other immigrants, they took part in a Westernizing process that resulted in their embracing values associated with being American; after all, they are—and always have been as much as any others—Americans. But unlike "white" Americans, who carry "white" values inside "white" bodies, Asian-Americans became "yellow" Americans who carried "white" values inside "yellow" bodies: a social contradiction. This may evolve into an impending psychological problem that will have no solution short of change in values by the dominant population. That change is very unlikely to happen considering that America tends to allocate wealth and power along racial lines. That is why values prevailing today suggest that Asian skin must eventually become "white," and the shape of the eye round, before the full rewards of society can be granted. That is pathological not only for Asians but ultimately America as a whole because it is unethical. That is not to discourage interracial marriages, but America should direct its energies against the prejudices that reduce interracial marriage to a contrivance of colonization. As that will require those inside the mainstream to change their values, Asian-Americans will continue to suffer the limited opportunities and quality of life reserved for those outside the mainstream.

At home and abroad, American influence drives the psychology of the Asian population. Asian-Americans have been no less susceptible than other people of color to the status hierarchy that approximates skin color bias. An effort to determine the existence of this bias among Asians was attempted by the author. Using a sample of college students, the following null hypothesis was formulated to provide a context for investigating the problem: "There is no relationship between skin color and selected values for skin color ideals." The sample conducted during 2000 consisted of 256 participants. Respondents had a mean age of 20 years. A self-report instrument available in Spanish was administered to Hispanics and English was utilized for Asians in assessing skin color. This instrument, the Cutaneo-Chroma-Correlate, was developed and previously pilot tested by the author to assess the relationship between skin color and various aspects of bias vis-à-vis sections "A", "B", and "C" (20). Section "B" (of the CCC) was used in this study to assesses the respondent's personal values pertaining to skin color. In differentiating responses, a designation of lightest was noted as 5, light as 4, medium as 3, dark as 2, and darkest as 1 (table 1).

Table 1 English

Section B	(A)5	(B)4	(C)3	(D)2	(E)1
	Lightest	Light	Medium	Dark	Darkest

Directions: Section "B" consists of 15 items designed to collect data on selected personal values. Using the codes above express your preferences by blackening in on the answer sheet the response which best describes your opinion. (A)-lightest, (B)-light, (C)-medium, (D)-dark, or (E)-darkest.

1 Pretty skin is
2 The skin color of pretty women is
3 The skin color of the men women like is
4 I wish my skin color were
5 The skin color of smart Asians is
6 The skin color of Asians who are snobs is
7 The skin color of Asians who are kind is
8 The skin color of my best friend is
9 I want my child(ren)'s skin color to be
10 My ideal spouse's skin color is
11 The skin color of my family should be

12 The skin color of my race (Asian) should be
13 The skin color of Asians who are physically strong is
14 The skin color of Asians who are dumb is
15 The ideal skin color of my projected child(ren)'s spouse is

Within their social environment, permeated by racial variation, Hispanics have been no less susceptible to that which approximates skin color bias. An effort to determine the existence of said bias among Hispanics was attempted. Using a sample of college students at one private and two public institutions, the following null hypothesis was formulated to provide a context for investigating the problem: "There is no relationship between skin color and selected values for skin color ideals." The sample consisted of 187 participants conducted during the 1997-1998 school year and selected from the registrar's roster. Respondents had a mean age of 20 years. Called the Cutaneo-Chroma-Correlate, this instrument was developed in Spanish and previously pilot tested to assess the relationship between skin color and various aspects of bias vis-à-vis sections "A", "B", and "C" (21). Section "B" (of the CCC) was used in this study to assess the respondent's personal values pertaining to skin color. In differentiating responses, a designation of lightest was noted as 5, light as 4, medium as 3, dark as 2, and darkest as 1 (table 2).

Table 2 Spanish

(A)5	(B)4	(C)3	(D)2	(E)1
Más claro	Claro	Medio	Oscuro	Más oscuro

Instrucciónes : Sección "B" comprende 15 categorias diseñadas para demostrar los valores personales del participante. Usando los códigos anteriores, exprese sus preferencias sobre los Puertorriqueños, marcando en negro en la hoja de respuestas la que mejor describe su opinión. (A)-más claro, (B)-claro, (C)-medio, (D)-oscuro, (E)-más oscuro.

1. Piel bonita es :
2. El color de piel de una mujer bonita es :
3. El color de piel del hombre que a la mujer le gusta es :
4. Desearía que mi color de piel fuera :
5. El color de piel de un Puertorriqueño inteligente es :
6. El color de piel de un Puertorriqueño presuntuoso es :
7. El color de piel de un Puertorriqueño gentil es :
8. El color de piel de mi mejor amigo es :
9. Quiero que el color de piel de mis hijos sea :
10. El color ideal de piel de mi compañero sería :
11. El color de piel de mi familia debería ser :
12. El color de piel de mi raza (Puertorriqueño) debería ser :
13. El color de piel de los Puertorriqueños físicamente fuertes es :
14. El color de piel de los Puertorriqueños ignorantes es :
15. El color ideal de piel de los compañeros de mis hijos es :

Results
Table 1

Item	1	2	3	4	5	N	MN	STD
20	4.0%	36.9%	57.5%	1.2%	.4%	256	2.57	.61
21	1.6%	20.5%	64.2%	13.8%	0.0%	256	2.90	.63
22	2.8%	52.4%	42.5%	2.4%	0.0%	256	2.44	.59
23	.4%	16.3%	75.5%	6.9%	.8%	256	2.91	.52
24	38.5%	27.5%	18.4%	7.8%	7.8%	256	2.19	1.25
25	.4%	6.9%	82.2%	8.5%	2.0%	256	3.05	.50
26	2.7%	19.2%	68.2%	9.0%	.8%	256	2.86	.64
27	1.6%	40.7%	56.9%	.8%	0.0%	256	2.57	.54
28	.8%	29.6%	62.0%	7.6%	0.0%	256	2.76	.59
29	.4%	24.3%	74.1%	.8%	.4%	256	2.76	.48
30	.4%	10.8%	84.8%	4.0%	0.0%	256	2.92	.40
31	2.0%	3.7%	46.7%	40.2%	7.4%	256	3.47	.77
32	17.2%	12.4%	33.9%	18.5%	18.0%	256	3.08	1.31
33	1.6%	29.7%	67.9%	.8%	0.0%	256	2.68	.52
34	.4%	18.2%	77.5%	4.0%	0.0%	256	2.85	.46

Table 1

As per item 1 most students (57.5%) responded "medium skin" when questioned about pretty skin. This was consistent with items 2 through 15 with the exception of items 3 and 5 (2]64.2%; 4]75.5%; 6]82.2%; 7]68.2%; 8]56.9%; 9]62%; 10]74.1%; 11]84.8%; 12]46.7%; 13]33.9%; 14]67.9%; 15]77.5%). When questioned about the skin color of the men women like (3) most responded dark: 52.4%. When questioned about the skin color of smart Asians (5) most responded dark: 38.5%. Referring to the aforementioned descriptive data it would appear with some exception (3, 5) that medium skin color is ideally valued among respondents.

Results
Table 2

Item	Response 1	2	3	4	5	N	MN	STD
1	68.9%	11.3%	6.6%	6.6%	6.6%	187	1.71	1.24
2	14.2%	20.8%	19.8%	20.8%	24.5%	187	3.21	1.39
3	13.2%	22.6%	15.1%	19.8%	29.2%	187	3.29	1.43
4	5.7%	7.5%	5.7%	30.2%	50.9%	187	4.13	1.17
5	5.7%	2.8%	10.4%	34.0%	47.2%	187	4.14	1.09
6	9.4%	8.5%	14.2%	23.6%	44.3%	187	3.85	1.33
7	15.1%	3.8%	14.2%	22.6%	44.3%	187	3.77	1.44
8	2.8%	4.7%	8.5%	31.1%	52.8%	187	4.26	1.00
9	2.8%	8.5%	8.5%	27.4%	52.8%	187	4.19	1.09
10	1.9%	7.5%	8.5%	30.2%	51.9%	187	4.23	1.02
11	3.8%	2.8%	9.4%	31.1%	52.8%	187	4.26	1.01
12	15.1%	21.7%	12.3%	17.9%	33.0%	187	3.32	1.50
13	18.9%	17.9%	8.5%	17.0%	37.7%	187	3.37	1.58
14	40.6%	11.3%	5.7%	17.9%	24.5%	187	2.75	1.69
15	42.5%	10.4%	22.6%	17.9%	6.6%	187	2.36	1.36

Table 2

As per item 1 most students (68.9%) responded "dark skin" when questioned about pretty skin. This was a contradiction to items 2 through 13. The largest response to these items was overwhelmingly "light skin" (2]24.5%; 3]29.2%; 4]50.9%; 5]47.2%; 6]44.3%; 7]44.3%; 8]52.8%; 9]52.8%; 10]51.9%; 11]52.8%; 12]33.0%; 13]37.7%). When questioned about the skin color of Hispanics who are "dumb" respondents overwhelmingly replied "dark skin" (14]40.6%). In glaring contrast the same students responded "dark skin" (15]42.5%) when questioned about the projected ideal skin color of their children's spouse. Referring to the aforementioned descriptive data it would appear with some contradiction that light skin is ideally valued among respondents.

According to these data, the presumption of a relationship between skin color and selected values for skin color ideals is plausible. Thus, the null hypothesis is rejected and an alternate accepted—there is a relationship between skin color and selected values for skin color ideals. Subsequent to findings are implications of a bias pertaining to the perception of various skin colors in the social milieu of the Asian and Hispanic populations that were questioned. These findings would appear to contradict—or at least challenge—the presumption of total group harmony and racial tolerance. Among Hispanics the color most often idealized was light skin. Among Asians the color most often idealized was medium skin. When Hispanics made exceptions for dark skin it was for "pretty skin" (20), those who are "dumb" (33), and the projected skin color of their children's spouse (34). When Asians made exceptions for dark skin it was for the "men most women like" (22) and "smart Asians" (24). In toto, while Hispanics more often idealized light skin in their responses, Asians more often idealized medium skin. In the context of colonization it would appear that exceptions are a reaction formation to the denigration of dark skin. That is, among Hispanics those who are dark are perceived as dumb, while at the same time, dark skin is the ideal color for skin and projected childrens' spouse. While Asian respondents considered the men whom women like and smart Asians as dark, all other responses were more often "medium." Of particular note between the two groups is the frequency of light skin as the ideal category among Hispanic subjects and the frequency of zero percent responses in the light skin category among Asian subjects. The most obvious cultural difference between the two groups is the predominance of Spanish among Hispanics and English among Asians. For both the significance of color implies a reflection of colonization in the attitudes toward persons characterized by dark skin. It is a bias that can be described as a variant of racism exhibited by the West toward all people of color. In the aftermath of dominance where "whiteness" is ideal, dark skin apart from medium/light becomes the standard of bias. The scores of Hispanic and Asian students, on section "B" of the CCC test, suggested their tendency for denigration of self and others on the basis of a minimal number of dark skin preferences. Such appreciation could be used to assess status and social worth, thereby contributing to the perpetuation of bias in an otherwise racially tolerant cultural environment. Conscientious observation holds potential for rescuing Asian-Americans at home and abroad from post-colonization. It will enable the incorporation and validation of new information. To the contrary, maintenance of colonial tradition and idealization of Western values discourages evolution of acceptance and new ways of thinking. The traditions of Western civilization too often defer to racial bloodline and nationality—the associates of skin color bias. As a result, Asian-Americans in an effort to assimilate and/or escape poverty at home have correlated skin color as the primary basis of bias. In fact, skin color bias is an ecological reality in the social milieu of migrant Asians and will become increasingly so in their victimization and quality of life. Their individual oversight is especially regrettable for other people of color who are similarly situated. What is more in the annals of history documentation exists that suggests social action—a mainstay of colonial freedom—precedes the resurrection of subjugated knowledge i.e. Asian tolerance (22). Asian-Americans are then challenged to decipher the maze of colonial tradition and create a suitable environment for the viable existence of the dark-skinned self. Efforts based solely upon merit in order to resurrect indigenous knowledge and values are critical to their psychological health, freedom, and ultimate quality of life.

References

(1) Loeb, R. (1970). The sins of bias. New York: Evans and Co., Inc.

(2) Williams, R. (1964). Strangers next door. Englewood Cliffs, NJ: Prentice-Hall.

(3) Delano-Buono, R. (1991). State repression and popular resistance: The criminalization of Puerto Rican Independentistas. Humanity and Society, 15(1), 111-131.

(4) Hall, Ronald E. (October, 1992). Bias among African-Americans regarding skin color: Implications for social work practice. Research on Social Work Practice, 2(4), 479-486.

(5) Hall, Ronald E. (1994). The Bleaching syndrome: Implications of light skin for Hispanic American assimilation. Hispanic Journal of Behavioral Sciences, 16(3), 307-314.

(6) Russell, K., Wilson, M., & Hall, R. E. (1992). The color complex. New York: Harcourt Brace Jovanovich.

(7) Montalvo, F. (1987). Skin color and Latinos: The origins and contemporary patterns of ethnoracial ambiguity among Mexican Americans and Puerto Ricans (monograph), San Antonio, Tx: Our Lady of the Lake University.

(8) Levine, E. S., & Padilla, A. M. (1980). Crossing cultures in therapy. Monterey, CA: Brooks/Cole.

(9) Felix v. Marquez, 78-2314, (U.S. Dist. CT. Dist. of Columbia, 1981).

(10) Stoddard, E. (1973). Mexican Americans. New York: Random House.

(11) Ibid

(12) Clark, K., & Clark, M. (1940). Skin color as a factor in racial identificaton of Negro pre-school children. Journal of Social Psychology, 11, pp. 159-169.

(13) Stoddard, E. (1973). Mexican Americans. New York: Random House.

(14) Ibid

(15) Kikumura, A. & Kitano, H. (1973). Interracial Marriage: A Picture of the Japanese Americans. Journal of Social Issues, 29(2), pp. 67-81.

(16) Banerjee, S. (1985). Assortive mating for color in Indian populations. The Journal of Bioscience, 17, pp. 205-209.

(17) Ibid

(18) Ibid

(19) Sung, B. (1990). Chinese American Intermarriage. Journal of Comparative American Studies. Fall, Vol 21(3), 337-352.

(20) Hall, R.E. (1990). The projected manifestations of aspira-

tion, personal values, and environmental assessment cognates of cutaneo-chroma (skin color) for a selected population of African-Americans. University Microfilms International, Ann Arbor, MI, 1-192.

(21) Ibid

(22) Foucault, M. (1980). Power/knowledge; Selected interviews and other writings. New York: Pantheon Press.

V

Eurogamy

Given the racial and ethnic shifts in contemporary Western cultures, scholars face an unprecedented challenge of keeping pace. The migration of Asian groups has created the need for a new and more inclusive world order. Of particular concern for the study of migrant Asians is to understand assimilation and how it is acted out via marital patterns. Heretofore little investigated, the growing number of migrant populations will be better served and will allow for a more comprehensive examination of sociological fact.

In a non-totalitarian society, certain forms of discrimination permeate its institutions. Scholars of the behavioral sciences refer to this as hegemony. Hegemony is characteristic of the West and other paternalistic cultures. It is a very subtle, but no less potent, form of discrimination. Among citizens of the West, hegemony fosters an "us" against "them" mentality thus reinforcing the skin color hierarchy. This notion of "us" against "them" may be the major component of culture from which, according to Welsing, the need to discriminate arises (1). It recapitulates itself at every level including what individuals might think of themselves. The color hierarchy has been thus all but ignored because it does not fit the rhetorical objectives of the dominant population.

Commensurate with Western assimilation Asians are regarded as "minorities." The most potent aspect of their identity as "minorities" is their relative dark skin. The issue of color has remained a significant part of Asian culture for quite some time. For Asians in their native land, it was enabled by British colonization, and, as a result, they internalized light skin as the ideal because they were powerless under colonization to contest the influence of the dominant Western population. But unlike that population, internalization of Western ideals resulted in psychic conflict because skin color is obvious upon sight. It is not only applied by Asians in the West, to assess the assimilation potential of groups, but by Asians in general to assess the assimilation potential of spouses as well (2). For all Asians, it is reflected in how they perceive attractiveness, who they decide to marry, and other life choices where skin color may be subjectively applied. Although it can be the entire process is not necessarily limited to Asians but apply to all people of color who migrate West (3).

Free and uninhibited assimilation would view the selection of marriage partners as an indicator that race, as per skin color or Asian eye shape, would not be a barrier. An alternate approach would infer exogamy as a function of inequality in dominant and racially stratified societies, i.e.: the West. For Asians who participate in exogamy, marriage then becomes a vehicle for the exchange of status characteristics (4). Similarly, Asians on that basis are presumed less eligible regardless be they of equal or higher socioeconomic status. Such thinking is a product of colonization. While some do marry people of color, Asian males who marry exogamously are less likely than is characteristic of females. This is in strict compliance with the implications of Western social norms.

Asian-Americans who marry exogamously (outgroup) do so in the midst of unprecedented social change. The "war bride" image, a stereotype of the humble, submissive Oriental mistress, is becoming obsolete. An objection to her traditional "war bride" mentality has undoubtedly influenced some to ignore the custom of endogamy (ingroup marriage). Furthermore, video technology and air travel have made it virtually impossible to remain isolated. When groups are isolated geographically, they are also isolated socially, providing fertility for ranking by skin color. As the West brings the world closer together via technology, social isolation—otherwise known as segregation—is viewed with less tolerance. The earlier isolation of Asian migrants hindered any effort at becoming comfortably assimilated into the mainstream of Western society. Access to educational opportunities and a better quality of life then suffered because assimilation was less forthcoming. Their unique features and "minority" status marked Asians as an imposition upon their host culture. Such imposition would not have been a consequence of normal assimilation as evidenced by the relative ease of the Western mainstream in accepting members from among the various European ethnics. The ultimate for Asians was instead limited access to the economic rewards of society and a quality of life commensurate with those limited rewards. It served as motivation for Asians to indirectly denigrate themselves via the internalization of Western ideals manifested in their patterns of matrimony (5).

Marriage, from the beginning, has stood as the true test and enabler of the colonial status hierarchy. But for members of European ethnic groups, being physically similar already located them on the upper levels of the hierarchy. That is, while Europeans experienced discrimination initially, assimilation required that they merely embrace Western ideals. For Asians, the decision to embrace Western ideals did not satisfy assimilation criteria totally. They were left with the task of somehow altering themselves to affect something less Asian or more Western. The difference in the process for European versus Asian ethnics then required that assimilation of Europeans be little more than the decision to learn a new language, practice new customs, or develop a taste for different foods. In most instances, by the second or third generation, they were fully assimilated into the mainstream of Western society. Thus, exogamy for Europeans was a result of the assimilation process whereas for Asians it became a strategy of making the concept of "eurogamy" (6).

The concept of eurogamy is a well-known phenomenon. The author originally coined this term. Eurogamy can be categorized as a select marital specific dictated by Western domination under the rubric of exogamy. It is the preferred marital pattern of a less powerful group, Asians, into a dominant group, Western male. In acquiring Western genes via marriage, the stigma of Asian skin color and features is altered in offspring. The idealized light skin and Western round eyes then qualify Asians for complete assimilation and the commensurate quality of life. It occurs most frequently among Asians who settle in large urban centers.

In New York City, Asians who marry eurogamously tend to be second generation or later, born in the West, female, older, better educated, of higher occupational status, and have higher incomes (7). Such urbanized Asians are associated less with the customarily closed Asian community. Whether or not their marrying eurogamously adversely affects their children has not been established as a fact of research, but, according to Sung, their children do appear to have problems psychologically (8).

For Asian-Americans who marry exogamously, the exclusive desire to marry men who have light skin is a dictate of Western assimilation and regarded as an invaluable asset in their quest for a better life. That qualifies European males as their spousal ideal. It further increases or reduces the frequency of exogamy between Asians and the various ethnics of color during the process of assimilation. It also necessitates that exogamy between Western citizens and migrant Asians having equal socioeconomic status be contingent upon the ability of the citizen via off-spring to lighten the skin color and Westernize the features of their Asian counterpart. It is most apparent among Asians migrating for the initial purposes of education. When the socioeconomic status between them and their potential spouses is unequal, an "exchange" theory based upon proximity to European light skin will be used as the selection criterion (9). The darker the skin, the more will be required in socioeconomic exchange. This is true whether either of the couple is immigrant or Western.

Eurogamy on the part of migrant Asians is also gender biased. For those living in urban areas the phenomenon is more obvious. For males the prospects manifest differently given the cultural tasks of Western assimilation. As a result, marital choices for both male and female Asians may be more impacted by the influences of Western culture because assimilation of less powerful groups into more powerful dominant groups frequently represents a form of colonization. In the Western tradition of the patriarch, that reduces the status of Asian males who are not members of the past or present colonial power structure.

By way of eurogamy, full assimilation of Asians becomes immediately accessible. In the process they may further internalize Western notions relative to dark skin, that discourage normal assimilation in toto. Such notions are quite common as reflected in the negative media portrayals of those descended from dark-skinned Africans. Other people of color who settled in Western nations, including those of African descent, might also harbor similar notions as pertains to skin color (10). All such persons understand that dark skin is regarded by the various Western institutions as an obstacle that might otherwise afford them an opportunity for assimilation and a better quality of life. Although eurogamy and the denigration of dark skin may appear illogical, in that it is psychologically counterproductive to the Asians who embrace it, historically these notions have been a strategy for the assimilation of migrant groups. In the aftermath, motivation for eurogamy is strongly reinforced.

As a social phenomenon, eurogamy is not without some benefit. While most people of color tend to congregate at the lower rung of the Western socioeconomic ladder, specific Asian groups enjoy one of the highest per capita incomes, including that of many Western Europeans. Those who aspire to assimilation dictated by Western ideals then internalize whatever ideals necessary without respect to the psychological and emotional costs incurred over time. Still based upon being people of color, Asian marital patterns are not commonly conjured up by mention of political activism. Their issues, as much as issues of other people of color, like equal educational opportunities and a better quality of life for their children—had a stake in the West's success. Like all people of color, in one way or another, Asians were prevented from becoming comfortably assimilated into the mainstream because they lacked the light, traditionally "white" skin. Access to educational opportunities and a better quality of life—regardless of eurogamy—has not been forthcoming for the group in toto. For that reason, marrying "white" as an assimilation strategy is ultimately pathological in some instances and life threatening, as in the following Asian case of Amanda (11).

According to a report in the June 1998 issue of *Gentleman's Quarterly* by Robert Draper Western eurogamy can lead to death. The poverty among specific Asians motivates them to migrate West seeking a better life for themselves and family despite the inherent risks. According to Western statistical data, migrant Asians in Australia are nearly six times more likely to be victimized by spousal homicide than are Euro-Australian women. Their circumstances have spawned a lucrative business venture in what has come to be known as the "mail order bride." For a fee the owners of such businesses will introduce Asian women in waiting to lonely Western "gentleman." Sometimes marriage results, sometimes not. However, given the lack of standard security measures every Asian woman who avails herself to the mail order industry puts herself immediately at risk for various kinds of abuse including death, as in the case of Amanda (names have been changed for confidentiality).

Amanda was a young attractive Asian when she first met Tom, a worn 46-year-old twice-married Euro-American from the state of Texas. Tom had four objectives in life: in his prejudice, he hated black men in particular; sex perversions were his passion; violence and his material possessions.

Tom had a history of exploiting Asian women for which every Asian woman is at risk. While stationed in Korea he was sexually exploiting both his American housekeeper and a twenty-year-old Korean woman to whom he had given financial support after meeting her at one of the local bars. She was young, petite and attractive. In her native Asian custom she was reared to believe that if a woman lost her virginity to a man she must devote herself, honor and obey him. Knowing this, Tom informed his young sex toy that he had murdered his unfaithful ex-wife and advised her never to tell.

It was in the November to December 1986 edition of the *Island Blossoms* paper that Amanda first caught Tom's attention. She was one of over 200 Asians listed. Her long dark hair and vibrant smile were symbols of natural Asian beauty. Amanda listed her age as 18 years old. She was 5'3" in height and weighed 105 pounds. She liked reading, movies and sincere gentleman over the age of 30. "Over the age of 30" was particularly impressive to Tom as he was well into his 40s. He would relocate Amanda to the U.S., provide her a home, buy her a new car, and send monthly checks to her family. Unknown to Amanda at the time was that she would also be the third of his wives to die a violent death.

From the start, Tom and Amanda's relationship was one that denied Amanda any sense of equality, given her poverty and youthful age. Tom had learned from various mail-order bride materials that it would take no more than a modest income to acquire the approval of Amanda's hand in marriage. He had done his research months in advance by scouring the mail order monthlies, looking for the perfect prospect. To her disadvantage, if Amanda decided to marry an Asian man she would incur little more than $3 a day of additional income and another body for the home to feed. Under such circumstances the children she wanted would ultimately suffer making Tom her only way out. Some of her closest girlfriends had already emigrated and found a measure of escape from the abject poverty that hung over her country. Tom owned a business in the U.S. and had recently qualified for a government pension. So Amanda did not object to her family having sent her photograph to be published in one of the mail order brides magazines. From the very start Tom used his wealth in every way to seduce the desperate Asian. He sent U.S. dollars in amounts that exceeded what her father earned in a month. He offered to move Amanda's entire family to the U.S. if she would be his wife.

Taken in by Tom's wealth Amanda agreed that he could visit.

Tom arrived with wallet in hand, all but forcing his entry into her home. Tom spoke to Amanda's father and reiterated his promise to send monthly checks to the family and relocate them all to the U.S. As is the custom, Tom dated Amanda non-stop for two weeks under the watchful eyes of a family chaperone. The chaperone had noticed an odd lack of charm in the man who had come compared to the charming letters Amanda had shared; he seemed to treat them all as if they were objects.

Eventually Amanda and the worn, charmless American were married. On their wedding night at a posh hotel, Tom managed a display of emotions that impressed his new bride, who would confide years later that making love to him felt like rape. She had realized that to Tom she was little more than a slave to accommodate his various sexual perversions. He was an avid fan of pornography as would be indicated by the boxes of tapes, vibrators, and dildos from previous encounters. Most hurtful of all for Amanda would be the men Tom brought home from his business to try out his new sex toy. Amanda was deeply offended by this, but learned later that Tom liked to watch.

After marriage Tom and Amanda traveled back to the U.S. Once they arrived, Tom informed Amanda that her primary function was "to serve me." She was then expected to be a quintessential parent, but not to the extent that parental duties conflicted with "serving me." Tom required Amanda to get up at 6:00 A.M. every morning. After she washed up she would attend to her chores and be prepared for his arrival from work that evening. Tom ordered Amanda further to wash her face at least three times daily and reply immediately to his verbal commands. Perhaps most denigrating of all was Tom's demand that Amanda have sex with him "at any and all times and with enthusiasm." For a few painful years Amanda endured these tragic circumstances until she was eventually found dead. Today Tom is serving a sentence for her murder.

Asian women who, like Amanda migrate West via eurogamy are in fact little more than objects. The idea that they are indeed regarded as objects is reflected in their treatment by the mail order magazine industry (12). One of the largest is *Cherry Blossoms,* which has grown about 10 percent in a succession of years. Its gross profits in 1997 reached nearly $1 million. Only young Asians are offered an opportunity to have their pictures advertised. Those over 30 are more likely to be discarded. A testament to this objectification is that since mail order businesses receive no money from the prospective Asian brides, women are treated like the commodities they are. Frequently discarded by *Cherry Blossoms* are Asians under 18 and over 45 years of age. The only difference between the treatment of women in the mail order business and those in prostitution is that one business is legal and the other is not. However, *Cherry Blossoms* and *Sunshine International,* both headquartered in Hawaii, do treat their girls with a little more respect than most.

In a given year thousands of Asian women post their photos with mail order magazines such as *Sunshine Girls* in hopes of migrating West via eurogamy. Similar to Amanda such women seek a better life for themselves with little protection from the dangerous risks involved, which despite *Sunshine Girls* involvement lurk nevertheless.

In an attempt to illustrate the extent of euragamy the author requested random samples of the magazine in brief for years 1991-2000 (one issue for each year). Listed were a total of approximately 620 girls ages from 18 to 30. The groups included Japanese, Chinese, Korean, Indonesian, Malaysian, and "other" to accommodate an occasional Russian, etc. For the most part race was not a significant aspect of the girls' requirement for correspondence. However, of those who mentioned race approximately 96% requested Caucasian men, 2% requested Asian men and 2% requested Hispanic men. The groups who selected Caucasians most were by far the Chinese (30%), the Japanese (27%), and the Koreans (14%). This would concur with the reputation of such groups as culturally inclined to human ranking by skin color hierarchy. Indonesian and Malaysian women, a much darker group, requested Caucasian as well (12%). Of the total Indonesian/Maylasian group one requested "no blondes please." As pertains to Filipino Asians posted in *Sunshine Girls,* 11% requested Caucasian men, and 2% requested Hispanic men. In the aftermath of colonization and otherwise Western world dominance it would appear that an increasing appeal of euragamy is progressively more forthcoming. Like Amanda many Asians migrate West out of necessity for themselves as well as family. In fact, they are thought to provide an economy from abroad without which many at home could not survive. According to Cecilia Hoffmann, a leading authority on female-exploitation issues, it is largely Asian women, rather than the males, who migrate West as so-called "overseas workers" (13). Such a term includes Asians who engage in eurogamy as Western housewives. Their contribution to the national economy amounts to 8 billion dollars annually (14). As a means to success by Asian standards, locals have thus institutionalized migration to Western households. This trend encourages Asian governments to ignore much of their welfare responsibility to the people, further encouraging Western migration.

In the more immediate sense eurogamy has appeal because domination is the preferred model of assimilation in the West. However, it requires a number of generations for the full genetic effect to become apparent in offspring. For first generation immigrants who settle in quiet, less urban communities, marrying eurogamously may not be as likely. In urban areas where it is more conspicuous, it may be referred to as the "Chung Phenomenon," after the Asian-American television journalist, Connie Chung. Asians refer to such persons as "banana"—an Asian who is "yellow" on the outside and "white" on the inside. Their eurogamy reflects an effort to become acceptable for assimilation and a rejection of social isolation brought about by traditional segregation.

Vis-à-vis the Chung phenomena the practice of eurogamy eventually results in what has been dubbed eurasian off-spring. A Eurasian child—part-Asian, part-European—might be viewed as having greater assimilation potential than an Afrasian child—of Asian and African parentage. The resulting skin color is a very critical factor, although not always a conscious one, for Asians who marry eurogamously. Furthermore, the "marginal" status of Eurasian offspring will make them more inclined to value light skin as more acceptable, because they may be but a shade from the possibility of sharing totally in the Western gene pool. Proof is in America's emerging eurasian population.

The United States 2000 census has made available an identity category separate from traditional race to accommodate Eurasian Americans (15). Hitherto, the Federal Census Bureau has yet collected data summarizing the Eurasian population. Consequent to criticisms from an increasingly vocal and active sector of the population, federal agencies have begun to modify standards for collecting race and ethnic data. However, such information remains unavailable for public consumption. Fortunately states such as California with a significant Asian population have acted with deliberate speed to accommodate racial changes.

In California a Eurasian person—i.e. biracial—is defined as one descended from more than a single racial category (16). Because maternal/paternal race data are organized by monoracial criteria, it is impossible to report the racial status of parents. Thus, the number of Eurasian births reported in the same data may be biased downward. Conversely, since racial status of children in the California data are derived rather than self-identified, it may actually overestimate the number of Eurasian births.

California today has one of the U.S.'s most diverse populations vis-à-vis immigration. While legal barriers to intermarriage were abandoned relatively early compared to other states, this has otherwise enabled little more than a moderate increase in Eurasian births within a 15-year period. However, taken as a percentage of state data in toto, biracial births—including Eurasian—rose from just under 12% in 1982 to just over 14% in 1997. In real numbers this increase accounts for about 50,000 births in 1982 and about 70,000 in 1997 (17).

Despite modest rates of increase, the number of Eurasian births in California is significant and substantial. In fact, biracial births exceeded that anticipated for the state of California in 1997 (18). The increasing size of this population provides a context for understanding the concerns raised by Eurasian Americans regarding identity. Identity conflict among Eurasians is a direct consequence of Western eurogamy.

When asked to identify themselves by traditional race categories, Eurasians are more often resentful or confused. All too frequently racial criterion has been utilized to categorize some who may subsequently experience serious identity conflict as white (19). As a result, it is incumbent upon associates to consult with individual Eurasians regarding their identity preference. They must be sensitive to the possibility that such persons may have experienced a dramatic change in social status attributable to the Western system of racial identification. Subsequent change can directly impact psychological well-being, self-esteem, interactions with others, and assimilation prospects.

Being Eurasian in the West requires/enables living a life of multiple identities (20). At the very least, said persons are the result of a predominantly black/white society that demands adherence to certain race-based social norms (21). Alternatively, today's less overt and more covert discrimination facilitates a separate Eurasian identity evolving its own set of applicable criteria. Being Eurasian then requires two processes: On the one hand, it may precipitate a conscious distancing from the stigmatized group—usually Asian descended. On the other hand, it may involve the creation of a new identity based in part upon an inability to be accepted without reservation by either composite race groups.

Living as a Eurasian person in a Western society demands identity diffusion in the traditional Eriksonian sense; at the same time, a Eurasian life may exemplify the functional identity of a "yellow/brown" or "white" citizen (22). Given their experiences, by the time they become of age Eurasians may be conflicted by identity (23). As per the stigma associated with Asian features, the ambitious confront major decisions pertaining to where they are going and how to get there. In a Western milieu that affects them personally they must prioritize Western values, standards, and ideals. The bright and talented cannot possibly ignore the inherent contradictions between those values, standards, ideals, and their personal lives. The middle class who may have been sheltered from such a reality, encounter stinging consequences by the time they reach adolescence.

As per Eurasians, eurogamy is a matter of the human condition that marriage to any potential mate is based on that person's ability to be not only perceived as attractive but particularly for males by females in a Western patriarch, a worthy prospect. But for many, knowing this has resulted in conflict about themselves, conflict about who they are, and most critically for Asians-American, conflict about their human worth as individuals. This response is not peculiar to Asians. All people of color—if they are at all perceptive—are quite familiar with this Western scenario. And in order to rationalize the resulting conflict, Asian-Americans in their high regard for children have come to perceive their own features as ugly and disgusting on the basis of their skin color and/or eye shape.

Asian-Americans residing in a Western environment are under constant pressures. As pertains to assimilation, their obvious differentiation is critical in the quest for self-acceptance. Particularly in the West, where the norm is a belief that superiority is physiologically based in a Western racial category, Asian features are denigrated. Any deviations of phenotype from the European race category are presumed inferior, enabling various social and political objectives. Accordingly, implications of eurogamy for the assimilation of migrant Asians are as follows: (A) concepts of superiority are continually rooted in the phenotype of a Western European ideal, although it is seldom articulated in polite circles; (B) by virtue of domination such concepts are incorporated into the Asian psyche as prerequisite to Western assimilation; (C) the effort of Asians to then assimilate has necessitated manifestation of the Bleaching Syndrome; (D) in its aftermath, surgical modification of the Asian eyefold and their eurogamous marital patterns enable a less Asian and/or Asian phenotype for a more Western look assumed to be commensurate with the canons of Western superiority.

In Western cultures a subcutaneous eyefold is perceived as germane to the phenotype of Asian populations (24). It presupposes interpretation as a peculiar phenomenon extended to those of Asian descent across historical era and geographical location. In the West, no other physiological trait so essentially defines Asian identity. Identity as evolution of social experience is well demonstrated in an analysis of the Asian eyefold, i.e.: small-eye phenomenon. Interest in this phenomenon among Western social scientists and physicians alike has peaked in recent years. Plastic surgeons in particular have been called upon to engage procedures that either inject or remove fatty cells, which enable the characteristic Asian appearance so critical to their phenotype and native identity (25).

Among Asian-Americans manifestation of a racial identity is a direct result of Western domination. Domination by Western concepts allowed for the exportation of racial values, which Asians internalized. As pertains to skin color, the uppermost in status were then accepted being light-skinned because they most approximate the dominant race groups. In an attempt to conform, Asian-Americans adhered to the racial prescripts of identity to enable potential assimilation. Their efforts facilitated a value system that is in many ways not only physiologically alien to them but psychologically brutal as well (26). The result is a configuration of identity whereby cultural and familial experiences are all but totally irrelevant to the assessment of identity. This being so, it is imperative to acknowledge the intimate Western associations between identity and power.

In the absence of power, the perpetuation of self-definition becomes ineffectual. Associated with power, Western ideals perpetuate the racial model of identity. As a logical consequence dominant race groups in the West maintain superior numbers, cohesion, and resources to sustain a European idealized identity system (27). Asians are more often victimized by their lack of power.

They may be short of numerical superiority but, in fact, are cohesive and share a common experience of identity ambiguity extended from the race paradigm—an ambiguity that has the potential to galvanize their numbers.

Subsequent to ambiguity, Asian identity vis-à-vis race in the West is generally regarded as rooted in culture (28). By lack of any biologically significant criteria, social scientists have determined race to be a matter of subjective interpretation. Thus, any biological traits that extend from identity based upon race may vary from one culture to another. Skin color, hair texture, and the like ultimately interact differentially to determine the identity of Asians who migrate West; therefore, identity is in fact a pliable cultural phenomenon. In the aftermath, Asians may be assumed to be racially diverse by any given system of identity. Thus, individual Asians can be simultaneously perceived in the West as European, Native, other Asian, and, in some cases, black dependent upon circumstances. However, an Asian identity that suggests African descent may be the most socially damning of all statuses for prospects of eurogamy or Western assimilation. Even then, to look white forces the same individual to identify as white to assimilate and engage a better quality of life.

Understandably some within the medical community are disturbed by the idealization of Western features. Social scientists are furthermore puzzled by the prospect of Asians who seek surgical alteration of an otherwise benign aspect of Asian physiology. They contend that emotional and psychological domination of Asians by an otherwise alien Western mainstream extends compelling influence (29). In an effort to assimilate into that mainstream vis-à-vis domination some among migrant Asians have engaged a willingness to modify one of their most pertinent physiological characteristics, enabled by the latest developments in surgical technology (30).

Data produced by various sources as to the rate of eye surgery among Asian-Americans is astonishing. According to a 1993 Hector and Gamble study, 26% of all Western women surveyed between the ages of 20 and 60 years old have sought alteration of their ocular regions by means of various surgical techniques. As pertains to those of Asian descent precisely, the AABA (Asian-American Beauticians Association) has determined that 95% of those women who seek surgical modification of the ocular regions have been of Asian ethnic origin (31). While such findings are not conclusive the assumption that Asian-Americans are dissatisfied with the appearance of their ocular region is not without merit. In an effort to justify otherwise groundless surgical procedures, some among Western medical and social scientists contend the Asian small-eye creates a driving hazard (32). That hazard subsequently manifests an endangerment to the general public safety. They contend further that subsequent ocular limitations necessitate the involvement of Asian persons in numerous traffic accidents otherwise avoidable were it not for the existence of their characteristic eyefold. To validate this assumption, amenable scientists have thus hypothesized that Asian-Americans do in fact harbor a gene deficiency that has extended the small-eye phenomenon for generations within their gene pool. It is exacerbated by their notorious endogamous marital patterns (33). While the merit of such hypotheses is conspicuously lacking and racist to say the least, those who support it have unfortunately managed movement into the arena of otherwise legitimate scientific circles.

While the aforementioned hypothetical rationale is factually inconclusive, some truth is evident in the consistent misrepresentation of Asian-Americans. Stereotypical depictions of those characterized by the small-eye phenomenon illuminate and/or dramatize the issue. Thus, while Asians are in fact a heterogeneous, multifaceted group they have been consistently portrayed in the West by the fabled small, slanted eyes of the various film caricatures. Furthermore, on the basis of being Asian-American such caricatures personify them as having tiny bodies, are "wimpy" guys and submissive girls (34). Representation of the entire Asian population via grossly distorted stereotypical images serves eurogamy and the emotional and social comfort of the mainstream Western psyche.

In fact, response to the Asian small-eye phenomenon is a defense mechanism that the West has utilized to marginally assimilate a group of people it is both uncomfortable with and threatened by phenotypically (35). That threat is most personified in the role of lead characters created by the Western film industry. Combined with the predominance of essentially European beauty standards the Asian small-eye phenomenon has come to represent something sinister, inferior, and unattractive in the context of what is acceptable.

One of the first Western films to exploit depiction of the small-eye phenomenon was produced in 1916 (36). It was titled "Fu Manchu." The lead character of the same name was portrayed as an evil, cunning, and diabolical figure distinguished by his obsession with taking over the world. It was released during the period of the Yellow Peril, thus it became extremely popular among the mainstream. To them Fu Manchu was a convenient scapegoat who rationalized and proved to satisfaction that the Yellow Peril was in fact a logical and valid conclusion to make of the Asian threat. The utility of this character culminated with the passing of Asian migration laws. In its place evolved another small-eye character no less stereotypical in its portrayal of Asian-Americans. His name was "Charlie Chan" (37).

Charlie Chan was a much less vilified film caricature than his Fu Manchu counterpart. He was noted by his exceptional intelligence and small, slanted eyes dramatized by a constant squinting expression. His frequent utterances of "Confucius say..." became an integral part of Western folklore. Unfortunately it also served as a conduit for denigration rendering Asian citizens the butt of jokes initiated by prophet like phrases. The lead character in the film series was at the same time wise and ridiculous but no less stereotypical. In an effort to accommodate the American psyche Charlie Chan and similar film series exploited the small-eye phenomenon via direct utilization of Asian characters however distorted. Modern day industries including advertisement have exploited same absent direct utilization of Asian participation altogether. Primary examples are evident among the various modeling agencies of the advertisement industry.

In an increasingly diverse racial environment, American advertisers of various commercial wares seldom use Asian models to sell their products. According to a 1992 survey of advertising statistics out of the hundreds of models maintained by the Wilhelmina and Ford agencies there were a grand total of no more than ten Asians (38). Asian males were not represented at all! In *Vogue* magazine 2.5% of its ads featured models of color in toto suggesting Asians as some percentage thereof. The same statistic for *Mademoiselle* was 2.6%. Furthermore, despite a huge market for the Oriental sexpot in Western nations only four Asian playmates have been featured in *Playboy* since 1988. Although these statistics suggest the low representation of Asians in the product sell industry recent trends have indicated an increase in media. Unfortunately some remain stagnant via their inability to accurately portray the "typical" Asian-American existent among the population. Their sinister characterization in film and the failure of the advertisement industry to employ Asian models at all is arguably a reflection of American beauty standards for which eurogamy is intended to compensate (39). In that context the characteristic small-eye phenomenon is perceived by Asian-Americans as an impediment to structural assimilation into the mainstream of society. Their apprehension is motivated by the fact that America does not differentiate between Asians regardless of ocular characteristics.

The act of marrying eurogamously among Asian-Americans continues to increase dramatically. While it was once considered taboo, and still is to many, of all recent Asian-American intermarriages most by far continue to be to Europeans. This means that only a relative small number are to people of color. If such rates do in fact reflect a dislike for dark skin among certain Asian-Americans, the psychological implications for off-spring of these marriages is not conducive to race relations or society. Given that the historical concept of "white" has been defined as "pure" the prognosis is discouraging.

Fortunately, with the existence of eurogamy as an extension of Western denigration in the social environment of Asian-Americans, their task is clear. As a group they must determine for themselves the worth of an Asian identity. Assimilation of all into the mainstream of American society must come as the result of an equally valued exchange of culturisms. In the aftermath the understanding of assimilation will be enhanced. The mainstream will then become more conducive and capable of assimilating its people in toto.

References

1 Welsing, F. (1970). The Cress Theory of Color Confrontation and Racism. Washington, D.C.: C-R Publishers.

2 Hall, R. E. (July, 1994). The bleaching syndrome: Light skin, psychic conflict and the domination model of western assimilation. The Indian Journal of Social Work, 55(3), 405-418.

3 Ibid

4 Ibid

5 Hall, R. E. (1997). Eurogamy Among Asian Americans: A Note on Western Assimilation. Social Science Journal 34(3), pp. 403-408.

6 Ibid

7 Ibid

8 Ibid

9 Ibid

10 Knox, D. (1985). Choices in Relationships. St. Paul, MN.: West Publishing.

11 Mazumdar, S. (1989). Racist response to racism: The Aryan myth and South Asians in the US. South Asian Bulletin, 9(1), 47-55.

12 Draper, R. (1998). Gentleman's Quarterly Magazine.

13 Sunshine International (Fall 2000). Kailua-Kona, Hawaii.

14 Ibid

15 Draper, R. (1998). Gentleman's Quarterly Magazine.

16 Census 2000 Complete Count Committee Handbook for Local Governments. (April, 1998). U.S. Bureau of the Census, Washington, D.C.

17 Tafoya, S. (2000). Mixed race and ethnicity in California. California Counts: Population trends and profiles, 1(2) 1-12. Public Policy Institute of California.

18 Ibid

19 Ibid

20 Tizard, B. & Phoenix, A. (1995). The identity of mixed parentage adolescents. The Journal of Child Psychology and Psychiatry and Allied Disciplines, 36, 1399-1410.

21 Mills, J., Daly, J., & Longmore, A. (1995). A note on family acceptance involving interracial friendships and romantic relationships. The Journal of Social Psychology, 129, 349-351.

22 Phinney, J. & Alipuria, L. (1996). At the interface of cultures: multiethnic/multiracial high school and college students. The Journal of Social Psychology, 136, 139-158.

23 Sowards, K. (1993). Assigning racial labels to the children of interracial marriages in Brazil: patterns in child mortality. Social Science Quarterly, 74, 631-644.

24 Tizard, B. & Phoenix, A. (1995). The identity of mixed parentage adolescents. The Journal of Child Psychology and Psychiatry and Allied Disciplines, 36, 1399-1410.

25 Sung, B. (1990). Chinese American intermarriage. Journal of Comparative American Studies. Fall, Vol 21(3), 337-352.

26 Hector & Gamble (1993). Examining the Asian-small eye syndrome. On-line: *http://www.pomona.edu/REPRES/Asians/ASIAEY.html*

27 Soule, S. (1992). Populism and Black lynching in Georgia. Social Forces, 71(2), pp.431-449.

28 Kitano, H. (1985). Race Relations. Englewood Cliffs, NJ: Prentice-Hall

29 Hall, R. E. (1997). Human development across the lifespan as identity model for Biracial males. Journal of African American Men, 3(2), 65-80.

30 Sung, B. (1990). Chinese American intermarriage. Journal of Comparative American Studies. Fall, Vol 21(3), 337-352.

31 Hector & Gamble (1993). Examining the Asian-small eye syndrome. On-line: *http://www.pomona.edu/REPRES/Asians/ ASIAEY.html*

32 Ibid

33 Ibid

34 Parrillo, V. (1990). Strangers to these shores. Macmiilian Publishers. New York, N.Y.

35 Hector & Gamble (1993). Examining the Asian-small eye syndrome. On-line: *http://www.pomona.edu/REPRES/Asians/ ASIAEY.html*

36 Kitano, H. (1985). Race Relations. Englewood Cliffs, NJ: Prentice-Hall

37 Weinstein, J. (1984). Fu Manchu and the third world. Society, 21(2), 77-82.

38 Ibid

39 Hector & Gamble (1993). Examining the Asian-small eye syndrome. On-line: *http://www.pomona.edu/REPRES/Asians/ ASIAEY.html*

40 Hall, R. E. (1997). Eurogamy Among Asian Americans: A Note on Western Assimilation. Social Science Journal 34(3), pp. 403-408.

VI

It's A Disease

Among the practical definitions, empowerment has been defined as an ability to gain power; to develop power, to take or seize power; to facilitate or enable power; to give, grant, or permit power(1). Torre further defined empowerment to be a process whereby people become strong enough to take part in, share control of, and influence direction of the critical institutions that impact their lives (2). Despite post-colonialism Asian-Americans must acquire certain skills, knowledge, and power to overcome a bias system based upon skin color.

The effort to empower became known as the grassroots movement. Asian empowerment is an American ideal capable of transforming the personal and professional lives of post-colonial individuals. The objective is to prepare those entering the mainstream to both assist others in utilizing their strengths and problem solve to reinforce self-reliance. The observant recognizes that Asian-Americans frequently suffer as the result of an inability to advocate on their personal behalf and thus feel powerless. In order to be effective in the lives of future citizens, scholars realized that Asian-American students must graduate from programs armed with the inherent sense of an empowered self.

Conversely, if teachers were to use dictatorial strategies to influence students and acquire power for themselves, they would be less than likely to foster an empowerment philosophy among them. The manipulation of others would undermine the broader objective of social change whereby Asian-Americans learn and play an active role within a democratic context (3). In accord with such a notion, as per Simon (1989), the literal meaning of "empowerment" is then to give ability to, or to permit (4).

Ashcroft further explains that an empowered person believes in his ability to act, and this belief will be accompanied by capable action (5). A challenge to the American democracy would be to determine what is fair in assessing its people and how their empowerment will be acted out in toto. Simply encouraging Asian-Americans to be good citizens and become activists in the broader sense without direction is pointless.

Similar to other Western democracies, Asian-American empowerment was little more than a failed attempt to redress power disparities in a multicultural setting. To remain viable Western standards at many institutions have been diversified. While disparities in power prevail, the current Asian-American population is at a much greater advantage in pressing for equal rights. Still many of the post-colonial checks and balances may today be passively enforced by race conscious administrators. Critics suspect such administrators violate equal protection and set up a process of reverse discrimination against Asian-Americans assumed in possession of power. They fail to acknowledge that a member of the mainstream population requesting power is not necessarily a victim and under the circumstances may be in a position to intimidate. What is more in a free society such as America it is difficult to deny opportunity to those who have the potential to bring about significant change.

The effort then on the part of Asian-Americans to empower themselves require a nation where its people interact on the basis of a shared respect (6). Although their roles differ, all are engaged in the process of civilization. The responsibility of citizens is to see to it that meaningful interaction takes place irrespective of race. For this to happen in a democracy, the nation must be a physiologically and psychologically healthy environment for people. Intimidation will make a sham of democracy. Above all, Asian-Americans should not feel inferior or powerless to differ with the mainstream. Exchanges by the end of the day should leave them feeling satisfied that they have learned and grown from the experience. That will allow them to approach subsequent issues with a feeling of empowerment and renewed enthusiasm. Thus, the quality of citizen relationships is of extreme importance if they are to be healthy and productive.

For Asian-Americans, the health implications of dark skin are manifested differently compared to the mainstream. Their personal disposition is a textbook lesson in domination. At one end of the spectrum is the light-skinned Euro-American so preoccupied with the dictates of power that his needs are limited by dysfunctions. At the other end is the despised person who for having been born dark is forever banished from the fold of acceptable. In an effort to endure pain Asian-Americans may delve totally into the world of suppression. They can know no mediation between mainstream bias and their health. In ways similar to other people of color their assimilation is jeopardized as well.

Western contact between Asians and Europeans began as the consequence of a differential in power. In the beginning these contacts were rigid and structured as pertains to sex, race, and various cultural prescriptions of appropriate behavior. Scholars have noted with keen interest the effects of such relationships but have done so in the context of race. The implications of skin color for health have lingered all but irrelevant. It is a consequence of the race-caste rhetoric that has neutralized the discussion of alternative models. In fact people of Asian descent who are poised for assimilation are socially and physically dissimilar in such a way that each group contains a full range of health issues. Some may ascend to the upper classes among their own. However accomplished, they are seldom accepted into the Western mainstream as bonafide citizens, and by virtue of their identification as "minorities" are prohibited from competing professionally except in token measure. But light-skinned Asian-Americans, unlike darker-skinned Asian-Americans, have not been denigrated to the same extent. For those who have lighter skin, the West regards them as less of a threat.

Where they participate in mainstream affairs they may excel regardless of their assigned inferior status. Consequently, many Asian-Americans have succeeded despite their differential treatment as minorities, but at a cost to their health. They have applied their skill and talents to become doctors, lawyers, and self made millionaires (7).

The dominant model of assimilation dictates what is healthy and what is not. Through Euro-American dominance, those who aspire to assimilate then alter in various ways aspects of self that the culture has deemed undesirable. In America, members of dark-skinned groups suffer reduced health status and self-esteem. That is not only true for America but, given its power, wealth, and media influence, often true of all people of color in the Western world context. When African heads of state are in need of economic assistance, it is the West who more often must volunteer financial support. That support is seldom given without expectations. In fact it is likely given, however subtley, in some manner that will ultimately facilitate the interests of nations lending support. For example, Cuba, closer geographically to the U.S. mainland than some of its states, receives no health aid dollars, while those in Guam nearly a world away are almost entirely dependent. Cuba is in political contrast to America while Guam could be regarded as an extension. Where nations choose to spend their dollar is a matter of choice and should remain so. The difficulty this presents, however, has to do with post-colonial dominance. Those nations composed of dark-skinned ethnic groups reinforce the assumed superiority of Westerners by too often being in a position of need. When one nation has a need that another can fulfill, the nation in need as a natural consequence will hold its suitor in high esteem. When it is more often the nations populated by dark-skinned ethnics who receive assistance from those populated by light-skinned ethnics, the stigmatization of dark skin becomes a cultural progression, even though it is assumed irrelevant. In this tacit context the dominant West may also export its values and ideals (8).

As per post-colonization America by population is defined as predominantly European and patriarchal, which defines dark-skinned Asian-Americans by racial dissimilarity and skin color as threatening. That threat necessitates their being singled out for various acts of brutality and other racist manifestations that impose upon health. But it is skin color, not the race of Asian-Americans, which serves as vehicle for racist acts. While people of color who are harassed by exuberant law enforcement officers are frequently identified by race it is arguably their dark skin that enables the assumed culpability, which dark-skinned Asian-Americans have complained about informally. Assumptions by law enforcement officers of culpability have sparked controversy and protest. In fact, assault of certain race citizens by law enforcement officers frequently has little to do with race and is arguably attributable to having dark skin, particularly where males are concerned (9). Skin color is the universal clue to race as those who commit racist acts do so on the basis of what they visually conclude about racial identification. The constant subjection of dark-skinned Asian-American males to racism in Western societies has become consequential to the physical health of all dark-skinned males. Among people of color it is manifested as a correlation between hypertension and skin color, making racism a disease risk for certain Asian males as men of color.

Medical research has established the fact that dark-skinned males live shorter lives than Euro-Westerners and are more likely to encounter significant health risks (10). For various reasons health care professionals have yet to list stress by racism as a cause of death. However, some health care professionals are beginning to acknowledge stress extended from racism as a health hazard on par with smoking and a high-fat diet (11). Among the day-to-day manifestations of stress that affect dark-skinned males in particular are those racist acts committed by various branches of law enforcement.

The physical health implications of racism, vis-à-vis law enforcement, among dark-skinned males are largely invisible to Euro-Westerners, many of whom see the complaints of such males as a function of what author Norman Podhoretz once described as "paranoid touchiness . . . ." (12). But recent police assaults—one fatal—upon two dark-skinned immigrant males in New York City form a distinct contrast in the perception of racism between the Asian- and Euro-Western communities (13). It is a contrast that permeates media as in the African-American New York case.

Prior to the age of technology, print media was the primary vehicle for communicating information. What people could not learn by word-of-mouth was left to what they could read, or what the literate could read to them. Although print was an established media, it was largely informal. This allowed the unscrupulous to incite for the purpose of increasing profits. In rationalizing the racist stereotype of dark-skinned males, print media profited by inciting. Such is evident in the New York case referred to as the Central Park Jogger (14).

Late one evening in 1996, an upper, middle-class investment banker was taking her daily jog through Central Park. The victim—a Euro-Western female—was violently attacked and raped by a gang of dark-skinned youths. The theme was old, familiar, and too often sensationalized by the media. It incited frenzy around the case by describing the accused as "animals" and a "pack." In an overt act of racism, print media managed to make the point of the perpetrators' racial identity via subtle implication and photography. Although this was not the first or last case of its kind in New York, it was a major story for local newspapers around the country. It was as if a message was being sent that the threat of the dark-skinned male was real and indeed unexaggerated.

The ability of print media to portray the dark-skinned male as racist stereotype has had quite an impact upon how he is perceived. That impact has only increased with the use of photographic technology. The camera has the ability to freeze a detailed likeness of the culprit, who could then be recognized on sight. Still motivated by profit, print media has used lighting, pose, attire, etc., to create whatever racist stereotype of the dark-skinned male it deems appropriate. The alleged defendants in the case of the Central Park Jogger were photographed in lighting that further darkened their skin and the solemn expressions on their faces made guilt seem all the more believable (15).

Following World War II television replaced radio in popularity. Its moving pictures brought images to life in a way that print or radio could not. More than any other component of modern media, television is by far the most potent vehicle for denigration. Since the advent of cable television, virtually every Western home has access to its transmissions. More so than print and radio, television is intimate. Its ability to drive home the racist stereotype of the dark-skinned male was politically exploited in the person of Mr. Willie Horton (16). Mr. Horton had been let out of prison where he had been incarcerated for rape. There was nothing new about this old stereotype, but the "virtual reality" of television allowed viewers to pseudo-experience Mr. Horton. It was assumed that Euro-American citizens, male and female, would then go out and vote accordingly. At any rate, George Bush, whose election team had exploited the stereotype, did in fact win the 1988 presidential campaign (17).

In a subsequent 1990 incident in Boston, Massachusetts, another dark-skinned male was accused of murdering a Euro-American housewife who was pregnant by her husband. The entire nation assumed the guilt of the accused based upon media hype and its larger than life photographs of the murder scene. Only after one of the accomplices involved in the frame-up came forth to reveal the truth, that the husband was the murderer, was Mr. Bennett—the alleged dark-skinned perpetrator—released from police custody (18). The belief that Mr. Bennett was guilty as charged was arguably, in large part, a reaction to his dark skin.

Because dark skin contrasts with the Euro-Western light skin norm, it is necessarily vilified in the subjective assessment of guilt, which is stressful and unhealthy. Dark-skinned males remain constantly aware of that assessment in all matters of public affairs. Vilification has contributed to the victimization of dark-skinned males as the racist stereotype who cannot conform to the light skin norms of mainstream American society (19). Hence, in comparison to those with lighter skin, dark-skinned males are, falsely accused as active participants in criminal activity more often than any other group. And given the power of media to impose and to monitor norms, such victimization may keep dark-skinned males who are otherwise ordinary law abiding citizens under constant emotional and psychological stress.

On the New Jersey turnpike a 42 year-old dentist has been pulled over by state troopers more than fifty times on his commute to work. Dr. X is not a careless driver. In fact, despite being frequently pulled over by police, Dr. X has never been issued a ticket. Each time the state troopers pull the dentist over the questions are routine: "Do you have any drugs or weapons in your car?" (20). Dr. X drives a gold BMW and is dark-skinned. For years dark-skinned males like Dr. X have complained about being humiliated by racist law enforcement policies without anything being done about it. The position of the police is that race is irrelevant to being stopped on the turnpike; but, in fact, skin color is the basis for being stopped according to three dark-skinned males— two African and one Hispanic-American who were shot by troopers.

As the four males drove along the turnpike in a rented van, police pulled them over and opened fire, striking three of the males and critically wounding two of them. At police headquarters officers contend the suspects were stopped because radar showed the van to be travelling at an excessive rate of speed. The department where the officers are stationed was forced to admit later that they had no radar equipment. The circumstances for the shooting are currently under investigation.

The most troubling aspect of this New Jersey incident aside from the shootings is the fact that no less than three years earlier a New Jersey judge concluded that troopers were practicing racial profiling. Instead of doing what was necessary to eradicate such racism from the ranks of law enforcement, the New Jersey Attorney General sided with the troopers to appeal the case. After the case reached public awareness, the Attorney General declined to pursue the case because of his concern for winning a political office.

It would appear, by the New Jersey case, that racism reaches every level of the Western judicial system extending to dark-skinned males a constant source of stress otherwise irrelevant to similar law abiding citizens. That the problem in New Jersey is so pervasive is exemplified by a decision of the United States Justice Department to intervene should the Republican governor decide to ignore it.

The constant stresses of racism experienced by dark-skinned males should come as no surprise because it permeates law enforcement policies. For example, the state of New Jersey eventually admitted that the State Police targeted dark-skinned motorists for drug searches during their travel along the New Jersey Turnpike (21). These tactics, while racist and unethical, are not irrelevant in Russia, where the KGB recruits members of the community to spy on its citizenry. In New Jersey, law enforcement has recruited motel workers to spy on patrons who speak Spanish or who pay their bills in cash. In New York, law enforcement denies the use of "racial profiling," but a recent story in *Crain's New York Business* raises serious questions (22). The newspaper interviewed twenty dark-skinned professionals who all gave detailed accounts of their experiences with racial profiling having been singled out and humiliated by police, usually for driving expensive cars.

This kind of continuous racism has deepened feelings of alienation among affluent dark-skinned professionals who had hoped that success would allow them to become bonifide Americans. But instead of fading into the Western patchwork, dark-skinned males have become an ever more popular target for law enforcement agencies. Their families bear a heavy burden in stress that keeps blood pressure abnormally high due to their male folk being targeted. Many are worried that fathers, sons, brothers, and husbands may one day be murdered by police officers convinced of racist stereotypes. Examples of what dark-skinned males including Asians experience in the post-colonial era are a threat to their health as a result of blood pressure diseases.

The medical measure of blood pressure is determined by the exertion of blood as the heart forces it through the body's arteries. One way in which blood pressure can rise is caused by the constriction of the arteries. This occurs in "fight-or-flight" crisis, as when a mouse suddenly encounters a cat. The sympathetic branch of the autonomic nervous system is stimulated and stimulation leads to contraction of the muscles of the arterial walls (23). The effect is analogous to squeezing a tube of toothpaste. There is an immediate increase in the force of paste being expelled from the tube. In the case of human beings, the skeletal muscle and the heart muscles receive increased supplies of blood, which is vital for both mice and humans when in the midst of a crisis situation.

Such extraordinary measures are all very well for mice attempting escape from cats. The escape does indeed require increased muscular effort. When it is over, the muscles inform the nervous system to decrease the blood supply, then blood pressure returns to normal. The situation is arguably different for dark-skinned males today. Seldom is there a crisis that would call for instant increase in muscular effort. But the fact that the lives of dark-skinned males are filled with any number of stressful racist situations mimics a state of permanent crisis. An unfair police stop and a racist court decision all trigger the sympathetic crisis reaction, even though a sudden spurt of muscular energy is of little use. But the human autonomic nervous system is not equipped with logistical apparatus. And so given the prevalence of racism, the blood pressure of dark-skinned males, without intervention, may remain constantly high, some more than others, but all to some extent (24). As a result, blood pressure is sustained at abnormally high levels, creating unnecessary health risks for dark-skinned males, which correlates directly with skin color. That increase in melanin (skin color) correlates with increase in hypertension rates among dark-skinned males. A decrease in melanin correlates with decrease in hypertension rates among dark-skinned males.

In severe cases, sustained autonomic exertion eventually takes its toll among dark-skinned males. Contributing factors include a gradual thickening of the arterial muscle walls. This, together with an increased sensitivity to stimulation, makes these wall muscles overreact to normal neural impulses. As a result, the wall muscles of dark-skinned males are in an almost constant state of constriction (25). The more constricted the walls are, the thicker and more sensitive they become. The end effect of this thickening cycle is hypertension. Symptoms of hypertension include headaches and dizziness. If serious and prolonged, the disease may cause lesions in the arteries that supply the kidneys, the brain, and the heart. This may result in eventual kidney failure, cerebral stroke, coronary disease, and heart attacks (26).

Hypertension is a by-product of sustained sympathetic arousal. Thus, dark-skinned males would expect its incidence to go up with increasing amounts of stress related racism. This is indeed the case as a matter of historical fact. For example, there was a marked increase in the incidence of hypertension among the inhabitants of Leningrad after the siege and bombardment of that city during World War II (27). Similar effects can be produced by the socioeconomic stress extended from racism that dark-skinned males encounter. Thus, hypertension is much more common among dark-skinned males being poorer as a group than Euro-Westerners; and it is especially prevalent in inner-cities marked by high population density, poverty, and crime (28). Still other studies reveal that hypertension is more prevalent among persons whose occupations impose stress. An example is provided by air-traffic controllers, especially those who work in airports characterized by dense air traffic (29).

In all of the aforementioned cases, the critical element differs from the stress mice incur from cats, but rather is the individual's reaction to it. Furthermore, what the besieged citizen of Leningrad, the dark-skinned male, and the overburdened air-traffic controller have in common is unremitting sympathetic stimulation induced by stress; they are all in a state of constant crisis and eventually their bodies exact a price in the form of hypertension. The difference being the end of war for citizens of Leningrad and job choice/change for air traffic controllers unlike racism suffered by dark-skinned males, which is not yet ended nor a matter of choice.

By definition, hypertension involves the excessive pressure of human blood against the arterial walls; usually restricted to the condition in which the resting systolic pressure is consistently greater than 160mm of mercury (30). Systole pressure refers to the contraction or period of contraction of the heart, especially of the ventricles during which blood is forced into the aorta and pulmonary artery. Its counterpart, diastole pressure, is that phase of the cardiac cycle in which the heart relaxes between contractions; specifically the period when the left and right ventricles are dilated by the blood flowing into them. Further definitive criteria of hypertension include individual complaints of symptoms commonly associated with it such as headaches and dizziness.

Hypertension in the dark-skinned community is frequently referred to as high blood pressure by common folk. While high blood pressure can occur as a consequence of physical activity, as when mice attempt escape from cats, hypertension is diagnosed when blood pressure climbs above normal, i.e. 160mm, and remains abnormally high regardless of emotional state and/or physical activity.

According to medical references, hypertension is a major public health problem in America (31). There are a large number of Westerners who qualify for the diagnosis of hypertension. Unfortunately, the burden of hypertension is not equally shared vis-à-vis racism. Dark-skinned males have the highest incidence of hypertension compared to any racial or ethnic group (32). Given the implications of medical research, it becomes compulsory that hypertension assume the status of a primary health problem in America.

In 5 to 10 percent of persons diagnosed with hypertension, specific organic causes can be identified. The remaining 90 to 95 percent are said to suffer from primary hypertension or the disease of hypertension. The major factors thought to play a role in the disease of hypertension are heredity, diet, especially the amount of salt in the diet, and stressful environmental factors that for dark-skinned males would include racism as well as social, economic and psychological factors. From the identical twin studies and family studies conducted by researchers, it is clear that heredity is key and may account for about 50 percent of the causes of hypertension (33). The role of racism and psycho/economic factors are difficult to study, but probably exacerbate factors in those persons already susceptible because of heredity and/or diet.

When considering hypertension in general, and controlling for family income, education of the individual, geographical region, and place of residence, the data shows that as family incomes go up the percent of persons with hypertension will decrease from 25.7 percent of those with income of less than $5000 to 11.8 percent when income reached $10,000 or more. As the level of education increases, the percent of individuals with hypertension decreases. Those completing college have approximately 40 percent lower prevalence rates of hypertension than those completing less than ten years of school (36.9 percent lower in dark-skinned college graduates and 41.6 percent lower in Euro-Western college graduates who are less likely to encounter racism). Two factors could attribute to this association: age and weight. Adults with less education are more likely to be older, due to the fact that years of education have increased for all sex-race groups over the years. But incidence of hypertension is not eliminated when age is controlled for. And the largest difference in hypertension between educational classes is seen in the younger age groups who may have more frequent and intense encounters with law enforcement officers. This difference is much more striking in dark-skinned males than in Euro-Westerners, especially among those younger than 50 years of age. Among the youngest dark-skinned males (30-39 years) those with a college education have a hypertension prevalence rate almost 50 percent lower than those with less than 10 years of formal education (13.7 percent vs 26.6 percent), and 40-49 year old dark-skinned males who are college graduates have hypertension rates almost forty per cent lower than dark-skinned males of the same age with the least education (25.2 percent vs 41.2 percent). A smaller contrast is found among 50-59 year old dark-skinned males. Only among dark-skinned males 60-69 years of age is there no clear gradient in the incidence of hypertension (34).

Hypertension is one of the most serious health problems of dark-skinned males in America today. One quarter of Americans who have hypertension are dark-skinned and about one dark-skinned male out of every four, age 18 and over, has it. The ratio rises to two out of five among dark-skinned males over 40 (35).

As per studies related to dark-skinned males, vis-á-vis skin color, the following is fact: skin color is significantly related to the diastolic blood pressure level in specially selected high social class groups. Why this association between skin color is shown with diastolic pressure and not systolic may be a chance occurrence or it may suggest more genetic control over diastolic than systolic operating only in the light-skinned, high social class group. There are other factors associated with blood pressure that are equal to or greater than the correlation of blood pressure with social class. Social class membership shows a difference in life styles, diet, mobility and preventative health behavior, all of which may be related to hypertension in dark-skinned males—but that skin color correlation is no less of a fact (36).

It has been found that more darker-skinned males have the tendency to develop hypertension than lighter-skinned males. It has also been hypothesized that genetic factors as manifested by skin color play an important role in the occurrence of hypertension among dark-skinned males. Thus, on the basis of skin color dark-skinned males, regardless of race, may live as a minority group within a minority group. Although little is known about the actual demographic distribution of dark-skinned males by skin color, their occupations, their income, and their educational levels, various survey data helps to fill in the gaps. However, this information is not always reliable, and cannot be easily compared with census data. Given these circumstances, dark-skinned males face various forms of racism not limited to law enforcement. Except in areas with large populations of dark-skinned males, the American populace is unfamiliar with the correlations between skin color and hypertension.

Acknowledging the correlation between skin color and racism is extremely important. In some ways, skin color forms the backdrop of experience for dark-skinned males, acting as a lens through which many familiar and community events are filtered. Russell, Wilson, and Hall explained well how skin color has important lessons for society, including doing work with other populations who have experiences similar to racism (37).

Few issues divide Western nations as much as power and racism and the questions of police misconduct. Auditing for both can enhance society's ability to measure racism and increase the effectiveness of laws designed to counteract it. As illustrated by the use of citizen's review boards, auditing's link to public policy is especially close. Because of this, documentation of racism such as that presented in the New York and New Jersey cases can influence the terms of the debate over strengthening laws, which will require a redistribution of power.

The ethnic, racial, and gender disparities in health status is well-documented (38). This disparity disproportionately effects people of color who suffer from higher incidents of mortality and morbidity. The increase of health problems among dark-skinned males in particular is a major public health issue. For example, the early onset of prostate cancer has become more common among dark-skinned males than any other ethnic group (39). As for those beyond 60 years of age, 71% have hypertension, compared to 60% for other populations (40). In addition, sociological hazards such as racism and discrimination have exacerbated the disparities.

The current problem with health disparities in large part emanate from power and findings that people of color have historically had a general mistrust of health services as well as the medical community. Largely fueled by the vestiges of institutional racism and the well-publicized, federally funded Tuskegee experiments, the response of people of color to public health concerns has been met with hesitation and skepticism. The disproportionate numbers of dark-skinned males affected by various health challenges, particularly those at or below poverty level, compromises the stability of the community and contributes to rising health care costs.

Despite communication efforts and technology, regular health assessments and screenings for prevention and early detection of disease are not routinely practiced in all communities. Some of the more popular communication models such as those for "stop smoking" campaigns, or for "drinking and driving", have been effective for the mainstream population, but less effective in off-setting the persistent health disparities between people of color and the mainstream population.

Disease prevention and health promotion are a critical part of public health efforts because of the potential to: (1) stop diseases from occurring, (2) detect existing diseases early in order to permit more effective treatment and avoid undesirable consequences, and (3) provide effective prevention and intervention of chronic or irreversible diseases (41). Through a health promotion initiative the direct delivery of health care can help to decrease morbidity and mortality rates by tailoring a disease prevention and health promotion program (42). However, for this to have a significant impact, an effective communication model must educate people of color regarding their health. This segment of the population has been labeled hard to reach, and has not been amenable to the type of prevention programs available to the mainstream population due to a lack of power (43).

Communication of disease prevention and health promotion information is equally critical to public health efforts because of its threefold implications: (a) broader audiences, (b) greater publicity, and (c) greater likelihood of changing behaviors and attitudes. While prevention and promotion are crucial elements of the health care process, many of the research interventions implemented today have been relatively small scale (44). There is a need for more health promotion and disease prevention programs that reach larger segments of the population (45). For example, community-based smoking prevention programs have greatly reduced smokers' risks of suffering from smoking-related diseases (46). However, many of these programs are concentrated within a small area (community schools, youth groups, and jobs) and fail to reach audiences across state boundaries. Conversely, some health promotion and disease prevention models have been disseminated nationally. For example, Jason developed one of the only effective large-scale media-based health promotion intervention models involving smoking cessation, drug abuse prevention, stress reduction, weight control, and HIV/AIDS prevention (47). This large-scale prevention effort incorporated multi-level, multi-component influences (e.g., media, parents, community leaders, school and government administrators). The outcomes indicated that the initiative was successful at decreasing student tobacco use, lowering family use of cigarettes, alcohol, and marijuana, decreasing reported stress levels and increasing student knowledge of how to reduce HIV/AIDS risks.

While Jason's model was designed to convey messages that can help people stay healthy longer; primarily middleclass, predominately mainstream populations participated and benefited most from such organized, formal communication models (48, 49). These health promotion and education programs have not significantly influenced people of color, particularly those who are socially and economically disadvantaged. But, there have been a number of initiatives that have been implemented to target this group. For example, several organizations in South Carolina designed programs to educate and screen men for prostate cancer however, they were somewhat ineffective because they had not taken into consideration the need to seek community involvement in the development and implementation of acceptable educational efforts. They found that taking a different approach by seeking community involvement and developing health education materials that were relevant to the community were effective. The message "Real Men

Get It Checked" dealt with the masculinity issues and encouraged men to get prostate screenings. The initiative turned out to be highly successful because an effort was made to gain an understanding of minority attitudes, beliefs, and knowledge about health and prostate cancer. Outreach materials, tools, and methods were constructed based on feedback from the minority community (50).

Historically, people of color have not responded to traditional health promotion interventions (51). Cultural traditions, lack of appropriate and timely information, past experiences with the health care system, perceptions of the lack of benefits of health promotion, environmental challenges, independent health-seeking behavior, and lack of gender-specific health care facilities have all been identified as factors contributing to low participation in existing health promotion programs (52). In fact, the culture of Asians and others is different from the mainstream culture and is often not well understood or investigated by those who plan health programs. For example, Asian-Americans are very communalistic and family-oriented. However, most health promotion and disease prevention communication models do not take into consideration the utilization of cultural mediums for integration into a model. If these initiatives are to be effective within the Asian-American community, it is critical that cultural mediums be considered and integrated into communication models.

Williams (53) found that the most successful methods for reaching elderly people of color was through the recognition and utilization of personalized and familiar sources existing in the community, particularly because they provided communal support. The findings in this study were consistent with one another study on people of color, which suggests that health promotion programs and campaigns are more effectively channeled through individuals and institutions important to the population's social network (54). Together, these studies suggest that there is a lay referral system from which many people of color seek advice about health matters. Within this referral system are family members, clergy, folk medicine practitioners, friends, and other community members.

Similarly, Williams found that the church is the most valued organization involved in outreach activities pertaining to people of color and is very influential in the decision-making process of many (55). The South Carolina initiative for prostate cancer (cited earlier) has given grants to 30 churches throughout the state for the dissemination of information (56). Other cultural gathering places such as community centers, barber and beauty shops, private homes, and schools were found to serve as cultural posts for outreach activities (57).

From the dearth of research and the utilization of small samples, it is evident that the culture of Asian-Americans is not always a primary consideration in the design of health communication models. Furthermore, the behaviors and attitudes of Asian-Americans are under-examined. For example, Freimuth and Mettger, found that people of color reported heavy use of electronic mass media and much less use of print mass media (58). Thus, today there is an over-reliance on health information via electronic media. As a result, people of color are overexposed to "ends" information (messages that increase what one wants to achieve) through television and radio, but underexposed to the kind of information largely available through print media that may help to achieve the desired result. In effect, people of color are locked into information "portals" where contact from the outside is limited and misinformation is prevalent (59).

Failure to consider culture in the development of health promotion and disease prevention communication models is not the only structural barrier that exists when working with minority populations. Gender has also been less likely considered in the development of communication models. Asian-American male culture is significantly different from female culture and is often not well integrated into health promotion/disease prevention programming. For example, research suggests that men are socialized to conceal vulnerability and to be independent, which has "acted as a barrier" in their health-seeking behavior (60). As a result, male patients are more likely to receive care in emergency rooms, utilizing such access as a regular source of care more often than female patients (61). Nevertheless, disease prevention and health promotion material is still channeled primarily through traditional health care facilities (e.g., doctors' offices, clinics).

Many of the increasing health problems today are not only due to access, but are largely influenced by a lack of culturally sensitive disease prevention measures and power. The research literature has suggested that acceptance of and participation in programs increases when the needs identified are similar to those perceived by the targeted population and when members of these groups are vested in planning program activities (62). "When people are motivated to acquire information and the information is functional in their lives, they will make use of it" (63). Thus, culturally-sensitive national communication models are needed that reach more people of color with health messages that could increase their awareness of risk factors for illness and increase their participation in health promotion activities.

As mentioned previously, Jason was successful at targeting national audiences with his media-based health promotion intervention model; nevertheless, he failed to utilize the numerous traditional institutions valued by the Asian-American community, despite his attempt at minority outreach in prevention efforts (64). While the media represents an excellent form to alert thousands of community residents to health promotion initiatives, it is equally critical that national health communication models utilize and exhaust the cultural venues utilized by the Asian-American community for effective communication.

As an unwritten policy, racism is covertly associated with societal institutions, including law enforcement, because it is an extension of post-colonization. Such ideas have become so ingrained that they override the possibility that health is an issue. No doubt as scholars have noted, democratic living is based on the balance between status and power. Certainly the effort on the part of dark-skinned males, including Asian-Americans to overcome racism is a legacy devoted to that ideal. However, the implications of skin color for health induced by the capricious pursuit of power will wear at the moral fiber of a true democracy. In order to circumvent chaos a way must be found whereby Asian-Americans can be valued despite the "minority" label. "When the value of either individuality or community significantly supersedes the other then the one which dominates distorts the democratic ideal" (65). In such an environment the philosophical traditions of America and the democracy under which it operates will be best sustained by uncompromised integrity.

References

(1) Hasenfeld, Y. (1987). Power in social work practice. Social Service Review, 61(3), 469-483.

(2) Torre, E. (1990). Drama as a consciousness-raising strategy for the self-empowerment of working women. Affilia: Journal of women and social work, 5(1), 49-65.

(3) Goodman, J. (1992). Elementary schooling for critical democracy. Albany, NY: State University of New York Press.

(4) Simon, R. (1989). Empowerment as a pedagogy of possibility. cf H. Holtz, I. Marcus, J. Dougherty, J. Michaels & R. Peduzzi (eds). Education and the American dream) 134-146). Granby, MA: Bergin and Garvey.

(5) Ashcroft, L. (1987). Defusing "empowering": The what and the why. Language Arts, 64, 142-156.

(6) Schreiber, M. (1987). The definition of the situation. The Jewish social work forum, 23, 11-23.

(7) Hall, R. (2001). Filipina Eurogamy: Skin Color as Vehicle of Psychological Colonization. Manila, Philippines: Giraffe Books.

(8) Kitano, H. (1985). Race relations. Englewood Cliffs, NJ: Prentice-Hall.

(9) Hirschman, C. & Kraly, E. (1990). Racial and ethnic inequality in the United States, 1940 and 1950: The impact of geo-

graphical location and human capital. International Migration Review, 24(1), 4-33.

(10) Michigan Public Health Institute, (1995). Challenges of a lifetime, 1, 11. Okemos, MI.

(11) Staples, B. (May 2, 1999). When the "Paranoids" turn out to be right. Times Fax, Editorial, p 8.

(12) Ibid

(13) Fried, J. (May 7, 1999). In Louima's first day on stand, he tells of brutal police assault. New York Times, A, 1(2).

(14) Goldman, J., Toth, J. & Tien, L. (August 19, 1990). 3 found guilty in Central Park Jogger attacks. Los Angeles Times, A, 1(2).

(15) Sullivan, R. (July 11, 1990). Videotapes are core of Central Park Jogger Case. New York Times, B, 3(2).

(16) Ribadeneira, D. (October 30, 1994). Like father, like son— Jeb Bush ad evokes Willie Horton. Boston Globe, 7(1).

(17) Bush, Gore and Willie Horton. (July 15, 1992). Detroit News, A, 14(1).

(18) Rakowsky, J. (June 30, 1995). Evidence pointed to black suspect, police captain says of Stuart case. Boston Globe, 78(1).

(19) Hall, R. (1992). Dark-skinned male stereotypes: Obstacles to social work in a multicultural society. Journal of Multicultural Social Work, 1(4), 77-89.

(20) Hosenball, M. (May 17, 1999). It is not the act of a few bad apples. Newsweek, 34, 35.

(21) Staples, B. (May 2, 1999). When the "Paranoids" turn out to be right. Times Fax, Editorial, p 8.

(22) Ibid

(23) Mosby, (1998). Mosby's Medical, Nursing, & Allied Health Dictionary, Edition 5.

(24) Ibid

(25) Beckett, A. (1983). The relationship of skin color to blood pressure among Black Americans. Atlanta, Georgia: Atlanta University.

(26) Lipowski, Z. (1975). Psychophysiological cardiovasular disorders. In Freedman, A., Kaplan, H., & Sadock, B. (eds.), Com-

prehensive Text Book on Psychiatry. II vol 2 1660-68, Baltimore: Williams & Wilkins.

(27) Henry, J. & Cassel, J. (1969). Psychosocial factors in essential hypertension. American Journal of Epidemeology, (90), 171.

(28) Lipowski, Z. (1975). Psychophysiological cardiovasular disorders. In Freedman, A., Kaplan, H., & Sadock, B. (eds.), Comprehensive Text Book on Psychiatry II vol 2 1660-68, Baltimore: Williams & Wilkins.

(29) Kochar, M. & Daniels, L. (1978). Hypertension Control. Saint Louis: Mosby Co.

(30) Mosby, (1998). Mosby's Medical, Nursing, & Allied Health Dictionary, Edition 5.

(31) Perry, M. (1983). Lifelong Management of Hypertension. Boston: Nijhoff Pub.

(32) Beckett, A. (1983). The relationship of skin color to blood pressure among Black Americans. Atlanta, Georgia: Atlanta University.

(33) Wilbur, J. (1977). Hypertension: An editorial. Phylon, 352-355.

(34) Beckett, A. (1983). The relationship of skin color to blood pressure among Black Americans. Atlanta, Georgia: Atlanta University.

(35) Perry, M. (1983). Lifelong Management of Hypertension. Boston: Nijhoff Pub.

(36) Beckett, A. (1983). The relationship of skin color to blood pressure among Black Americans. Atlanta, Georgia: Atlanta University.

(37) Russell, K., Wilson, M. & Hall, R. (1992). The color complex: The politics of skin color among African American. New York: Harcourt, Brace, Jovanovich.

(38) DAG Online (2000). Vital Statistics on the web.*http://www.afroamerhealthdata.com/vital.html*

(39) Carpten, J. (January/February, 2000). A broad view of prostate cancer: What do we know? Minority Health Today, v 1, 2, p 16-18.

(40) Douglas, J. (January/February, 2000). Pathophysiology of hypertension and its impact on treatment of the minority population.

(41) German, P.S., Fried, L. P. (1989). Prevention and the elderly: public health issues and strategies. Annual Review of Public Health, 10, 319-332.

(42) Braithwaite, R.L., Murphy, F., Lythcott, N., & Blumenthal, D.S. (1989). Community organization and development for health promotion within an urban black community: a conceptual model. Health Education, 20(5), 56-60.

(43) Williams, M.P. (1996). Increasing participation in health promotion among older African-Americans. American Journal of Health Behavior, 20(6), 389-399.

(44) Jason (1998). Tobacco, Drugs, and HIV Preventive Media Interventions. American Journal of Community Psychology, 26(2), 151-187.

(45) Schreiber, L. (2000). Overcoming methodological elitism: Afrocentrism as a prototypical paradigm for intercultural research. International Journal of Intercultural Relations, 24(5), 651-671.

(46) U.S. Department of Health and Human Services (1997). Smoking Cessation: A Systems Approach, Agency for Health Care Policy and Research (AHCPR).

(47) Jason (1998). Tobacco, Drugs, and HIV Preventive Media Interventions. American Journal of Community Psychology, 26(2), 151-187.

(48) Ibid

(49) Lacey, L., Tukes, S., Manfredi, C., & Warnecke, R.B. (1991). Use of lay health educators for smoking cessation in a hard-to-reach urban community. Journal of Community.

(50) Ross, H. (September/October, 2000). Prostate Cancer: "Real Men" are checking it out in South Carolina. Closing the Gap. Washington, DC.: Office of Minority Health.

(51) Williams, M.P. (1996). Increasing participation in health

promotion among older African-Americans. American Journal of Health Behavior, 20(6), 389-399.

(52) Ibid

(53) Ibid

(54) Yee, B. & Weaver, G. (1994). Ethnic minorities and health promotion: developing a culturally competent agenda. Generations, 28(1), 39-44.

(55) Williams, M.P. (1996). Increasing participation in health promotion among older African-Americans. American Journal of Health Behavior, 20(6), 389-399.

(56)) Ross, H. (September/October, 2000). Prostate Cancer: "Real Men" are checking it out in South Carolina. Closing the Gap. Washington, DC.: Office of Minority Health.

(57) Williams, M.P. (1996). Increasing participation in health promotion among older African-Americans. American Journal of Health Behavior, 20(6), 389-399.

(58) Freimuth, V.S., & Mettger, W. (1990). Is there a hard-to-reach audience? Public Health Reports, 105(3), 232-238.

(59) Ibid

(60) Reisberg, L. (2000). Colleges start clinics for doctors-averse men. The Chronicle of Higher Education, July 7, A39-A40.

(61) Berman, B.A., Yancey, A.K., Bastani, R., Grosser, S.C., Staveren, A., Williams, R.A., & Lee, D. (1997). African-American physicians and smoking cessation counseling. Journal of the National Medical Association, 89(8), 534-542.

(62) Williams, M.P. (1996). Increasing participation in health promotion among older African-Americans. American Journal of Health Behavior, 20(6), 389-399.

(63) Freimuth, V.S., & Mettger, W. (1990). Is there a hard-to-reach audience? Public Health Reports, 105(3), 232-238.

(64) Jason (1998). Tobacco, Drugs, and HIV Preventive Media Interventions. American Journal of Community Psychology, 26(2), 151-187.

(65) Goodman, J. (1992). Elementary schooling for critical democracy. Albany, NY: State University of New York Press.

VII

What Asian-American Women Say

Asian woman A is an attractive well-educated mother of two. Her husband is a physician and works at a Michigan hospital. They met in college and emigrated to the U.S. about eight years ago. They live in an upper middle class neighborhood. Woman A is very Asian in appearance with lighter brown/yellowish skin. She is a little larger in stature than most Asian women and speaks with a subtle accent, but otherwise has good English.

Q: Ms. A, I would simply like you to tell me about your home in Asia and I guess I should repeat again that by taking part in this interview that you agree to cooperate. That I'm not paying you or otherwise inducing you to take part other than of your own free will. And the first question I have is would you tell me about your home in Asia?

A: O.K. Um, our family lived in a small town which is about 15 minutes away from a more populated area and we lived in a ranch type house which had four bedrooms and we had servants, like two servants in the house. There were also in the house four of us children and my parents, O.K. Um, O.K. what are they?

Q: Did you say you had servants? Did you say you had four servants?

A: No, two servants.

Q: Well, you must have been fairly fortunate.

A: I guess so because my Mommie was a doctor and my father was an engineer.

Q: O.K., so you come from a very educated family?

A: I guess so.

Q: Yes, yes, very educated.

A: Education was very important.

Q: Yes, it is one of the things I learned in Asia that I think it is a traditional part of the culture that the parents educate the children.

A: Yes.

Q: O.K.

A: Although on my visits it appears that sometimes people don't get jobs after college.

Q: Yes, I encountered a lot of people with college degrees in Asia working in department stores.

A: Uh, huh, right.

Q: Yes, yes. Well, how did you come to migrate to the United States?

A: Actually, it was through my husband. I'm the only one in my family who lives here because my husband . . . my husband's Mom was a U.S. Citizen and she was petitioned by a son and so everybody, everybody was here already. My husband was working in medicine.

Q: Oh, O.K. Are you in medicine also?

A: Yes. In our country.

Q: O.K.

A: So, the difference is I no work now because I have three kids. Actually I could practice medicine if I wanted despite a lot of tests...I passed them already, you know I passed them in 1994. I have to go far away places or whichever hospitals that accept me which, in our case, we don't want to be far away from each other so either I look for a hospital around here who will accept me or I will stay home with the kids.

Q: Your husband is Asian also?

A: He is.

Q: Was he born in the same area?

A: Born in Asia. The same area where I was born.

Q: O.K. Now what university did you attend?

A: The University of _____ and then we separated and I went to University _____.

Q: I've heard of it, yes.

A: And my husband went to uh. . . our _____.

Q: I've heard of it, yes.

Q: I understand that the University of _____ is supposed to be the top university in Asia.

A: Yeah, but supposedly they are very selective, but some people you know those with money kind of like have their sons or daughters admitted because of their connections. Not always, but it does happen.

Q: Ms. A, can you tell me a little bit about your marriage and your family life? I guess you were married in Asia?

A: Yes, O.K. We were married in Asia 10 years ago and, uh, but he was here, uh, as an immigrant, my husband. So he just had to go back and marry me. And then I was left behind with myself and my family and then he came back and I got pregnant so he came back to visit the little one and he went back again to the United States and I was alone with my parents and my family.

Q: So, you have sisters and brothers?

A: Yeah, I have two sisters and one brother. They're all there.

Q: What do they do professionally?

A: Yeah, my, uh, the youngest one is an engineer, the second one is an accountant, she works in the bank, and the eldest one he also work in the bank. He's in business administration. He's finished college.

Q: So, your parents would have accepted nothing less than to have their children very well educated?

A: I guess so. It is very common.

Q: One of the things that I noticed as an American visiting Asia is that women seem to have a little more freedom in that culture than they do in this culture. Or they seem to be a little more respected. Do you think so? Asian women seem to be respected more by Asian men than American women are by American men.

A: Oh, I think so, yeah. Uh, we, uh, that is part of our culture, women should be well respected by men. I guess we expect it here to be that way when we came in here.

Q: Oh, but one of the things in the United States is that Americans don't really want their doctors to be . . .sort of don't want their daughters to be doctors and engineers and it seems to me that in Asia their families encourage their daughters to be whatever they want to be.

A: In Asia?

Q: Yes.

A: I guess not. Like my parents encouraged us to be more like them, doctors or engineers but they don't force us; they just encourage us and things like that. I don't believe that they really want women as doctors, they just let you choose whatever you want. They don't force us, but they encourage us.

Q: O.K.

Q: So you would say that if we were talking about the Chinese... the Chinese were never part of the colonial Asian experience. Would you say that the Chinese have more status or prestige in Asia now?

A: Than the same people here?

Q: The people in Asia.

A: Since I was born... I never experienced the such people here. It's like mostly Chinese. I don't have. . .oh, probably in the South, uh, in the so-called certain area there are more light-skinned people.

Q: What about prestige is. . .is there a kind of lifestyle associated with lighter skin like the mixed population? Or the pure lighter-skinned Asian?

A: Among some of the older ones especially living in the area. That would include the Chinese who are everywhere but concentrated in the downtown area.

Q: O.K., yes I did see a lot of Chinese in the area and as I said they seem to be a very viable business community. One of the things that impressed me, and you mentioned mestizo, is the variation in skin color and phenotype. You're a doctor so you're familiar with the term cutaneo variation as it relates to human skin. And in the United States we have a lot of variations as well. We call Asian a very heterogeneous population. I don't know how Asians think of themselves, but I sort of see them as a heterogeneous population to the extent that you have people who are very, very dark-skinned and people who look Caucasian. Not very many, but there are some who look Caucasian so I'm wondering if you could tell me anything about the implications of skin color in Asia—how people react to it. You've been here for seven years so maybe you've noticed that skin color is very important here. It's not something that people talk about but it's something that everyone understands, and you not being what's called Caucasian looking yourself, I'm sure that there are things and experiences that you've had in the United States because you would be considered a minority here or a person of color. I'm sure there are experiences here that may not have been. . . how should I say it. . .pleasant experiences. Can you say something about the issue of skin color in Asia?

A: In Asia?

Q: O.K.

A: Mestizo… that means you are mixed, more fair, you aren't white but you aren't dark.

Q: Basically, I understand that mestizo basically means mixed and some people will be mixed and they will be lighter-skinned and some people will be mixed and they will be darker-skinned. And I also noticed in Asia there were people there who were Asian and Arab mixed as well.

A: Oh, yeah.

Q: You don't see very many, but there are Arab and Asian mixtures and so they have a different kind of skin color.

A: But I don't think color really matters in Asia because most of us are like a mixed breed. Even if you are dark you look pretty and you maybe, how do you call it, educated or kind . . . but there is no color or racial discrimination what you call it. Because most of us are kind of the same except for some mestizos who are mixed, but we don't look at them as if they pure like, uh, the fair, I mean darker or mixed it doesn't really matter about skin color as long as. . . . I don't know if money is very important, but, uh, most of them look the same and even if you are not educated . . . even if you are white, I mean light, light colored, but uneducated it's not good.

Q: Yes, I didn't get the impression that when I was in Asia that there was really color discrimination like you have in the United States, but I thought I kind of got a sense that maybe when it came to beauty for example. . . the prettiest women were idealized as light-skinned because they were fairer skinned.

A: Right, yeah, when you consider mestizo they like just to look at you because you're beautiful because you're mestizo. Oh, yeah, yeah, what you said is true. When you're like more white . . . when you're lighter-skinned you're very pretty even if you don't really look that pretty.

Q: Right, but if you're dark, and I saw so many very dark-skinned. . .what I thought were very beautiful Asian women and they had this pretty smooth dark brown skin, but they didn't seem to think that they were pretty.

A: Yeah, I guess, I think so. Uhm, I don't know. . . it's pretty complicated even if . . . some of us consider not so black not so dark pretty as pretty.

Q: What is pretty to you—hair?

A: Yeah. I guess, and deep set eyes like more on the white side.

Q: O.K., now how does. . .what's the implication of skin tone for men? They like women to be fairer. Is that true of women for men? Do Asian women like fairer men also?

A: Uh, huh, that's why we are afraid to get too dark. . . in the hot sun because we might get burned and then the men won't (laughter) want us.

Q: No, I know men like Asian women to be light-skinned, but I am interested in Asian women . . . the women, what kind of men do they like?

A: Oh, oh, darker men.

Q: They like the darker men?

A: The darker men.

Q: Do you think this skin color preference has more to do with what men like or what women like? I mean, do light-skinned Asian women see themselves as beautiful because that's what the men like or that's what the women like?

A: I think that's what the men like.

Q: That's what the men like. Now, do the darker-skinned men think that they're better looking or is it that the Asian women think the darker-skinned men are better looking?

A: They think that women like darker-skinned men.

Q: O.K. Do you have any idea what that comes from? Where do you think that came from?

A: It probably . . . had something to do with the word macho thing...macho is part of being a man.

A: And then a lot of people talk about the ideal man...they call it tall, dark, and handsome.

Q: Yes, yes, they say that in the United States.

A: Oh, over here?

Q: Yes, yes.

Q: O.K., do you think that there is any relationship between a person's skin color and their education or their income?

A: No, no.

Q: So, you could be very, very dark and be wealthy and be very light and be very poor?

A: Yes. You could be very light and not so good looking and be rich or educated.

Q: O.K.

A: There's no difference.

Q: Which do you think is more important to Asians—a man's looks or his income, his earnings?

A: For us? For me?

Q: From the Asian's perspective, yes. What do you think you value more in a man?

A: The money (laughter)

Q: Oh, it's just like in the United States?

A: Yeah, even if he looked ugly you know the money counts.

Q: One of the things that I've noticed as an American in review of the literature that I've done and visiting Asia you know about the mail order brides—you've heard about that?

A: Oh, yeah.

Q: There's magazines that have pictures of Asian women and then you buy these magazines like if you live in the West. . . they sell them in Australia, United States, England and if you see a picture of a young Asian woman that you like then you can write this magazine and they will sell you her address and you write them. Now, one of the things that I've been concerned about and one reason I'm writing this book is because some Asians have been exploited and hurt as a result of it. They get letters from guys who are really not eligible, to make a long story short. And one of the things I've noticed is that 95% of Asian women who are mail order brides. . . they intermarry with European westerners and I was wondering was that by intent or was that by coincidence?

A: European westerners you mean from here in the west?

Q: Well, in the United States you have a lot of different people. You have Hispanic men, African American men, Asian men, and European men and in Australia you have similar types of men, but one of the things I found in my research is that of those mail order businesses I'd looked into and those magazines that advertise mail order brides over a span of 10 years from 1991 to 2000 one of the things I found is that 2% of the Asian women requested Asian men, 2% requested Hispanic men and then 96% requested European or Caucasian men. Now, I was wondering what's the significance of this? Why do they do that?

A: Uhm, a lot of people I've heard have as a dream to have a husband who is white so there's a mixture of dark skin and they can become white.

Q: O.K.

A: So it might be that if there is a white husband at home or a wish to have a husband who is white or Caucasian then we can have a mestizo or mixed daughter or son.

Q: And if the daughter or son is lighter then they would be prettier?

A: Prettier, yeah.

Q: O.K. That makes sense. I thought maybe it had to do with the fact that Caucasian men are recognized as being more wealthy, more powerful or something like that.

A: I think . . . yeah, it's something to do with that too because they consider whites . . . they think that the whites are more educated especially when you come to the U.S.

Q: Yes, yes, and by your living here you know people think everybody here is rich and you know that there is a lot of poverty here.

A: When you see somebody who's like Caucasian or American a lot of women like want to flirt with him.

Q: O.K. Now, I find that Asians I encounter in Asia have a different way about themselves than the Asians I encounter here. The Asians here—and I don't now if I had seen you at the university that I would have been able to tell if you were Asian unless you told me because you could pass for Hispanic. If so I wouldn't have known you were Asian but one of the things I noticed about Asians in Asia is that they were extremely kind. . . extremely courteous and extremely personable. I mean it's like I've never seen people act as nice . . . maybe it was because I stayed in a big really fancy hotel and they thought I had a. . .maybe they thought I had money. No, but I mean just in the malls people were very nice as well.

A: Yeah, generally

Q: Yes, yes.

Q: O.K., well we were talking about the skin color in the mestizos. One of the other things that interested me when I visited
   Asia is that I see people of color all around the world as having
   a lot in common in their political and economic circumstances
   particularly as it relates to the West and specifically the United
   States. One of the things that I learned of Asian history in
   studying for this book is that when the United States was at
   war, there were black soldiers stationed in Asia as part of the
   American military and one of the things I found out is that
   you had a lot of African-American soldiers who were fighting
   for the U.S. who deserted the Army, deserted the U.S. military because they refused to fire on Asian soldiers because they
   felt the Asians, number one, were being unfairly treated because they had been colonized, and, number two, a lot of black
   soldiers felt there were too many Asians who looked like them.
   And they had difficulty firing on dark-skinned people and so
   some not only deserted, some joined the Asian military and
   that story has never ever been told.
A: Yeah.
Q: It's a little known fact. I read it in a book . . . it may have
   been a dissertation. I pulled a lot of dissertations at Michigan State that were written by Asians about Asia. And I
   either read that in one of those dissertations or a book that
   I was able to find, but that's something that I'm going to
   delve further into because there may be a story there that's
   been sort of well hidden but I'm interested in knowing
   what you think or in knowing . . . what you can tell me
   about your identity as an Asian and how you relate that
   identity to the rest of the world and to other people of
   color, Hispanics, African-Americans, Native- American
   people here they call them Indians, and other Asian people.
   How do you. . . . what are your political philosophies or
   political views with regard to, you know, some of the difficult. . . the racial difficulties that we're having in the world.
A: Uh

Q: In the United States or anywhere in the world wherever you choose to comment.

A: Uhm, obviously there are stereotypes when we're talking about Asians we think that there are news from Asia and mostly bad news.

Q: O.K.

A: That's what we hear or what we read in the newspaper and I kind of have sympathy for the Asians even if you know we say we are great . . . of course, people always say we're great . . . I mean like you, you say you're great and we want to be proud of ourselves. Seems like very small things that we can be proud of. Uh, that's why maybe we flee from our country and went . . . went away because we want to have a better future. We want to show, uh, to make the most of what we can do and if we are there in Asia I'm not sure if we can do the best that we can . . . or we can be compensated for what we are working for. So, that's what we are faced with as part of ourselves. You can do it, that is overcome the stereotype maybe not it is very difficult even if you work very hard you still find yourself being discriminated against and you feel bad because you're not compensated fairly for what you do.

Q: How have people treated you here? Do you notice that they treat you any differently because you are Asian, in your work. . . .?

A: Actually, I just work a year . . . my husband doesn't tell me anything about being discriminated. Uhm, he is nice because he wants to be treated nice then he treats others as if it is something like maybe we should not be too sensitive to those issues because we just want to work. That's what we do in Asia, we just work hard, work hard to earn a living. Even in school I just work, that's it or I just talk to the teacher, but I don't complain.

Q: Do you think, have you gotten a sense from your husband that maybe he's considered different? Do they ever challenge his skill as a doctor? Do you think that they think he's not as good a doctor because he comes from Asia or. . . .?

A: Well, maybe, that's what I felt before actually; that's why I didn't want to go someplace where I could just be accepted because I wanted to be respected where I was to be. If you don't want me there after all I can do for you, you don't want me here that's fine. Sometimes, yes, my husband will feel challenged. Well, he does what he can and so far nobody complains so, but sometimes he makes a mistake and he just laughs it off and learns from it. Of course, people make mistakes, but he doesn't feel bad about it and he learns from it.

Q: Yes. And how long has he been a physician in the United States?

A: He trained for five years then he is working now at Sparrow like eight years.

Q: What is his specialty?

A: Pathology.

Q: Pathology?

A: Yeah. But he will feel bad because he worked so hard and then the elderly ones, you know the heads of the department, they put him down because he was like training. And you have to work hard and study, but he doesn't mind it. He just say O.K. I'll study harder. And then he just learns from his mistakes.

Q: Sounds like he's very, very secure in his position, his field.

A: Yeah, he likes it. He's actually is head of his department—he supervises a Jew, another is Chinese. But he had a resident who is also black. They get along.

Q: So when the kids are getting ready to start school do you expect to start practicing, maybe going back to work?

A: Uh, me? Yeah, my son he only 1-year-old and I would for sure.

Q: So, so, does your husband ever come home and since you're a doctor also ask you questions of what he should do or was this right? Does he ever refer to you?

A: Yes, now and then.

Q: So you have more or less like an equal relationship?

A: Uh, huh. Except he uh expects me that I don't know more in pathology so. . . .

Q: Well, that's his specialty.

A: Yes, that's his specialty so he doesn't ask me those questions.

Q: That's good. That's good. O.K. Ms. A, that kind of concludes my interview. I would only ask if you had any other questions or comments that you would like to add before I end this interview?

A: Uh, I just hope I get to read your book.

Q: Oh, O.K. I shall do my best.

Asian woman B is a middle-aged mother of three school-aged children. She emigrated to the U.S. about fifteen years ago. Her husband is white and they live in a lower middle-class neighborhood. She is dark-skinned, small in stature with very straight, dark, black hair, cut just above the neck. Her English is less clear but it does not impair her ability to communicate.

Q: The first question is that I want to ask you to talk a little bit about your home in Asia as much as you remember.

A: Yeah, uhm, O.K. actually we have two locations, the first part that I grew up in was _____.

Q: _____?

A: _____

Q: _____, I'm sorry. Yes.

A: Yeah, you know already why they called it _____ right?

Q: Well, I know a little _____ so I'm assuming it means . . . well, Negritos little Black that's the original Asians.

A: Yeah, O.K. Miguel's father is from Portugal. My great-grandfather, actually my grandfather, was born in Portugal and he told us that when we were young . . . his Dad used to be the shepherd and a butcher so during this time he taught him to cook, butcher like when there is trouble or something like that. I grew up in a small city. Actually my parents is from one of the _____ islands. Then they migrated to Negros at the time because of the sugar cane plantation. Uhm, my Mom . . . she didn't finish high school. My Dad wanted to be an engineer and because of problems at the time he become the secret foreman to the national government. He built bridges and my brother is the ones that rebuilt our city hall.

Q: O.K. It sounds like he was a pretty important person then?

A: Uhm, he's just a good person. In fact, when we were young I keep asking myself about my friends because when we were young we lived in the richest part of the whole city where all the people are rich. You know, for me to be rich and to live in that part of the city we come to the conclusion just because of my Dad that's why we lived out there. But because he was an alcoholic the neighbors tried to get us out from that place, that's why we moved to the secluded place of the city. This is like a suburb of the city and we lived at the back of the river. It's a nice place to live, but everything changes.

Q: Now, _____, and I assumed that they call it _____ because most of the people in the area are very dark, is that true?

A: Mmhm, actually in the Occidental the majority is Negros because we are dark-skinned people. Uh, the Oriental actually they divided the island into Negros Occidental and Oriental. I heard that some of my family just like my brother-in-law I knew that the forefathers were like Negritos because they're short and they got curly hair, but if you can look back at our history some of the dark people in our island they came from a certain tribe in Africa. I don't know which one.

Q: They call them pygmies.

A: It is something like that but this is part of the tribe of Africa that some of our forefathers came from, you know. But they said that when they traveled they saw Negroes. When the Spanish got over to Asia they said that mostly the pygmies are in Negros, you know. So, we called them that. And my grandfather said that the Oriental is separated from the Occidental because the Oriental they are dark skin but they are taller than the Occidental so that's why the Spanish separated them from those on the other side of the mountain. That's what they said.

Q: Yes, I want to at some point when I visit the island to get to meet some Negrito people because I'm very fascinated by them and the little bit that I've read about them. Can you tell me a little bit about your migration from Asia to here in the United States?

A: Yeah, uh, actually I came to my Mom, my parents. O.K. The first person that came over is my sister. She is living in Illinois and then the whole family decided to emigrate to the United States, since each and everyone doesn't want to, one went to Germany. Then my mother arranged for us to come here to the United States. It was difficult, but I finally decided to come here in United States, that's when the Marshall Law was declared so. . . .

Q: Marshall Law?.

A: Yes, supposed to be a long time ago I see her, but because of the Marshall Law at the time Marcos doesn't want us to come here so finally my brother-in-law got sick my Mom used to go back and forth to visit. I cannot get any promotion on my job so I finally decided to come here and help my sister. I think that's one of the reasons why I came here to help my sister out. I couldn't get married in my country so that's the main, main reason why I came here in the United States was to help my sister.

Q: So, what kind of work do you do?

A: O.K. uhm, back in my country I have a bachelor's degree in medical technology. Uhm, right here in the United States I could only get jobs at Burger King. Yeah, that's right I worked at Burger King and after two weeks I met the director at the hospital where he asked me to work for free so just like after two months of working for free at the hospital he hired me so I work as a lab technician for a while. I work now for three years and then I met my husband.

Q: Can you tell me a little bit about your marriage and your family here?

A: O.K., yeah. Uhm, my marriage with my husband was a problem—he is divorced. My religion does not like divorce.

Q: Catholic you mean?

A: Yeah. Very religious people. Uhm, in the first place my father doesn't know about getting married in a different culture. He thinks I'm just innocent about the American culture that he doesn't want me to get married to an American. The second part is that X is divorced and according to our faith, it is not accepted by our religion. You know, like my Dad was against the idea I married somebody that had been married. So, uhm it's a long battle and me getting married here in America is extremely hard. I really didn't expect that I would get married to a divorced guy, we are Catholics and coming from a family like mine was really hard. Just like X had to go to the classes, we had to study to be a Catholic, then we had to annul his marriage you know, and we had to wait for like . . . almost more than a year before we get married because it goes from the Cardinal to the Bishop and then from my parents, you know it's a long process. My family come back again, you know.

Q: Well, I'm a little confused because the impression I got during the times I've been in Asia is that the Asian people and certain Asian cultures were very tolerant with people who were not necessarily of the same race or the same religious background. They simply accepted people for who they were and the cultural issue didn't seem to be too prevalent there.

A: You're right. But my parents are very different.

Q: Very strict. O.K.

A: Very different. Because when my father learned that I want to come here in the United States he said it right away what you gonna do? You know, his impression is that when you go to the United States all you could learn is that . . . O.K. Asia at the time were so backward compared to the city. . . were too far.

Q: O.K.

A: Yeah, so just like people darker here we don't have nothing to do but go to church, go to the movies where in big cities like there's a lot.

Q: Yes.

A: I admitted to you that because I have my small town ways my Dad put me in the Women's University with all women.

Q: _____Women's University?

A: Yeah.

Q: I've been there. I've been there.

A: In the past?

Q: __WU is what you call it.

A: Yeah, 5th Avenue, that's where I went for my review. It's really a good school to review, but because they're all women this was my first time away from home.

Q: And they have to wear uniforms, too don't they?

A: Right.

Q: Yes, they wear uniforms.

A: I really hate that but anyway that's where my Dad put me just like since I came from a place where people were so backwards compared to the city. One day our guide took us to some park in the city, you know you can see people hugging, kissing and it's just like we're in hell and I'm sorry but that's the way I feel. I feel like oh my God look what these people are doing.

Q: Yes.

A: Are they scared of doing that. It's just the first impression that came to my mind that it's like I have a bad feeling inside me. I get upset. I can't understand why you know like why are they doing this? You know, because in our culture the way that we were brought up something like that should be done in the bedroom and nobody could see you not to be exposed. This is first time that I was exposed to sex and it was like Oh my God you know it's like uh you know. It's just scary. It's a scary feeling you know.

Q: Well, the city is pretty sophisticated and in fact I think there's more to do in the city than there is in Lansing. It can be a pretty sophisticated city at times. Tell me a little bit about the people. I assume you watch television and watch movies here in the U.S. Who are some of your most popular movie stars or entertainers that you like?

A: Uh, actually my number one is Denzel Washington, I like him. Uh, what's his name?

Q: Mr. T, he's the guy with the Mohawk?

A: Yeah, because Mr. T used to be a bar tender before he become famous. I would like to mention my black friend, my best friend she used to be one of his relatives and sometimes she asked me to go to her church so I did.

Q: This must have been in Illinois, I think that's where Mr. T is from isn't he?

A: Yeah.

Q: Chicago area?

A: Yeah, Chicago. He got his own church down there before. What his name . . . the other guy he's from Chicago too uh . . . .

Q: An athlete?

A: One in the Ghost Buster.

Q: Ghost Buster, Parker, Ray Parker?

A: No, no, no. What his name, uhm, you know. . .

Q: Gil Morrison?

A: Bill Murray.

Q: Bill Murray, yes, yes.

A: Yeah.

Q: He's a good comedian. He's a good comedian.

A: Yeah, but I used to watch him all the time. Of course, you're from Chicago you know the actors you have to follow it.

Q: I've heard, yes. In terms of women in Asia, since I've been going to Asia women there are some of the most beautiful and prettiest I've ever seen and I've been to Hawaii and Puerto Rico and all over but I noticed that all of the women there are so attractive that it's not anything unusual. So, they're extremely nice. All of the people are extremely nice and extremely warm and extremely friendly. What do you think is considered an attractive woman in the Asia? What's the Asian woman's idea of an attractive woman?

A: O.K. Uh, number one mystery. . .the smile, attitude, uh most of the time the hair.

Q: What kind of hair do they like?

A: O.K. Uh, most of the women in Asia, uh, O.K. they always have long hair, very shiny and I don't know why but you know sometimes the idea about women having a nice hair even when I was in Asia like I didn't want to discuss this with my husband because I think he was attracted to me because of my hair and the hair, I think the way we smile, the way you accommodate people. I know that in this country men like women in Asia because they're clean. Cleanliness you know. Which is true but I look at the guy like my husband. The first time I met my husband it turned me off because he got a dirty way about him and I just like clean.

Q: O.K.

A: I think something uh. . . .

Q: What about the skin color? Do Asians like women to be light?

A: I think so. I think so, because, uh, we did in our country. I didn't think we cared. But for me just like in Asia, uh, the discrimination in the U.S. is within the wealthy and the poor.

Q: The class?

A: The way you know you mingled where, and with whom. It doesn't always count about your skin color, it's your money. You have a car or something like that. In fact, I have a sister that my daughter-in-law's husband you know he thought that my husband came from Africa because his skin is darker than you. I came to United States my sister was eager to tell me that when you go to America please look for Michael Jackson because he looks a lot whiter you know, but. . . it's O.K. there's nothing wrong with that color of the skin in our country because in _____ alone most of the people there are dark skin except for some city folk that are down there.

Q: So, you're saying the lighter-skinned people are still kind of separate and apart from the population?

A: Yeah, in our island, yeah, there's still an area down there, they're all different speaking people. They're white.

Q: Oh, and do they. . . do they mix with the Asians or do they stay separate? Is there any kind of segregation?

A: Uh, they have their own ways, they mix when it comes to school, but when it comes to like community they have their own. Actually they are landlords or related to the landlords.

Q: So, there is kind of a class and maybe they, do you think that they may look down on darker-skinned Asians at all or . . . ?

A: Yes, uhm, before that's what I think, that they look down on people like me or something like that, but you know people told me before that that's what they did but when I went to the nursing school and the first time I went to college I went to nursing school in fact I think two or three of them came from that community that we went to school with, uhm, we thought we looked really like hired hands because they were lighter-skinned, they were richer than us, but uh when at school it doesn't matter if you have brains so it's like we're even, they have money but we darker Asians have brains.

Q: Do you mean to say they're not as smart as Asians?

A: Yeah.

Q: Do you think it's sort of like it's almost if they're lighter-skinned, that they usually have more money, usually are better off, or is that just a coincidence?

A: Uh, coincidence because they're some people who are darker-skinned too, but they have money just like my in-law, they're rich but you know they're darker-skinned.

Q: So, the light Asians there you say they have their own community so you don't really have any of them marrying dark people?

A: Uh, mostly these people seem to get married with each other that's what I noticed. They cannot marry their workers that is all I know. They cannot marry their workers. Uhm, they can marry somebody like them or somebody with some other high society people belonging to the high society group in Asia.

Q: So, if you are a native to your area and a very dark Asian but you are say a doctor then they cannot marry with the light or the light-skinned wouldn't intermarry with them?

A: Uhm, used to be I don't know now but before now we can't. Even though you are a doctor or something like that . . . you don't mingle because they cannot go to the hospital. . .they have their own hospital that they go to.

Q: Oh, then they're really separate communities.

A: Yeah, it's just like . . . O.K. in that hospital all the light-skinned they have a doctor of their own that just like the doctor that delivered them to their society something like that. To end up in that place is so different, you know. I know my cousin went out with one, the son of the landlord I know uh he was in love with my cousin before because my cousin got the lighter skin. They are attracted to somebody with the lighter skin and with the pointed nose.

Q: Yes, more European features.

A: Yeah, my other cousin used to be like that before because uhm his Dad is pure European and something like that. My Dad was the same way, I mean, the attitude is so different. My Dad's family there they're lighter skin just like they're so different now I mean my Mom's she is small. She is small and darker skin. I think that maybe that's one of the reasons why he doesn't like each other.

Q: Oh.

A: I don't know. That's what my feeling is and that Mom never say anything because I grew up without knowing that I still have my grandfather. I grew up I still have my uncle. I grew up I still have my relatives without knowing that I still have a cousin on the father's side. You know, and only in the middle part of my life that I found out oh I didn't know I still have a grandfather and something like that you know because maybe they were ashamed to make us family.

Q: Yes.

A: Yeah.

Q: You know that's where they're having all the problems. I was just there and I think my friend just told me recently that our leader has forced the people in _____ to release the hostages and they're supposedly negotiating now. I wanted to get to the area, but because of the problem in the southern area of the country I was advised not to go there. So, I'm going to make that the next trip. The last question I would simply ask you is can you say a little bit about your identity as an Asian? Do you feel more . . . well, the term is Asian woman for an Asian woman, I think they say? Do you feel more American, more Asian, or sort of like in between and what language are you most comfortable with, the native language or English?

A: O.K. Uhm, the way I feel right now is that uhm I mean the family boundaries with my belief about raising my kids the way my parents raised us, you know. And then American way maybe food, culture, you know, but I would like my kids to be exposed to much more.

Q: How do you feel people have treated you here? How do Americans generally treat you? Do they accept you? Are there any problems that you've had?

A: Honestly speaking, I was in Chicago I never did anything bad. My husband is white and sometimes it is different for him, but sometimes at work it's the same. My best friends they're black and you know I have my best friend her husband is black too. I don't care about skin but when it comes to work I think Chicago is much more better than here in Lansing because in Chicago when I was working down there, there is a lot of minority especially I work in the black community where people respected you as what you are and then they give you what you give to them. That's really my heartache. That's the only regret that I really have. I told my kids I hope that what I am experiencing right now won't happen to them because you can see my kids they're not white. You can tell that they're brown, you know. I work with the State of Michigan. Many times people make me boss to train whites when they hired them. When they hired somebody white they told me oh she's only a temporary worker you know. You didn't have to be a temporary worker because if there is money we can hire you right away. Something like that. I have a husband and a family. I cannot afford that, O.K. I train them and after six months they promoted her. The third one, you know, I was down there when they selected her. I did a fine job, you know. I'm the one working for this job, the supervisor left, I took over his place, working his work, doing his work, the same technician work. Then they hired somebody. I was down there when they said that nobody is qualified, but my boss came over I just trained them. I mean, if the person were going to be with you 8 hours per day for 2 weeks of training it only means they can be boss.

Q: That's training, right?

A: I don't know so. But for me just like of course I have to share him, this is what I'm doing, this is the way we do spectrogram, you know, you're feeding them. And then the last one is that you know I was applying for that and then they told me that I don't have a computer background. I working with the machine all the time, all they have to do is . . . if I don't have computer background why did they have to send me to school to learn computer? I didn't want them to just let me sit and not do anything with the computer but that's the question. That's the only thing that I sometimes really dread you know I was telling my kids that's the only thing that really America is not fair to minority. It's not really fair.

Q: Yes, yes.

A: My husband can see that. I cried. And my husband was telling me, too, O.K. when you was in the Army, he's a surgeon right. And my husband is trying his best that I could mingle with all the people he's working in this department you know. Just because my friends are minority because they dark you know and then I asked him how come that this so unfair that they even have a degree in criminal justice he become a surgeon while you, you still a correctional officer, you know. I'm not a member of the Ku Klux Klan, that's why.

Q: Yes, that's very common unfortunately, even if you're not a minority and you're a Caucasian and you have too many minority friends that probably works against you in a lot of cases. So, you see that's why people are so sympathetic in a lot of ways. They're very friendly, but you're right when it comes to the job and the economics it's very difficult.

A: I know.

Q: Well, Miss C, I really appreciate the opportunity to talk to you and I'm going to be including this information that you've given me in the book. I think maybe your friends told you I'm writing a book on Asians and I'll be identifying you by letter. I won't mention the names or any personal information. The lady who is publishing the book is an Asian living in Asia so it's an Asian book company.

A: What's her first name?

Q: I don't remember her first name, but her last name is _____ and she lives in _____. That's how I met her. At least I can look it up in my book and I wanted the opportunity to work for her because she is an Asian rather than mainstream and I'm not doing it for the money, I'm really doing it just as a service to the people and kind of an interest of mine.

VIII

Model Minority Gangs

Tied to the perception of Asian-Americans throughout the world is the "model minority" Eurocentric stereotype. This stereotype is a sociological demonstration of racism. The stereotype of Asians is questionable on methodological grounds. It is clear that social science cannot remain effective if it is continually subsumed by Asian stereotypes (1). Hence, in the conduct of social science research, it is imperative to consider re-evaluation of how Asians are viewed. Succinctly put, effective research in an era of increased racial diversity will require significant modification of methods (2). Supposed modification will allow for deviations from stereotypes and similar constructs deemed less relevant. The aforementioned re-evaluation is best illustrated via analogy.

An Asian and European are obviously similar in genetic structure: both frequent a common existential space, and both rely upon nourishment from the environment of that space to evolve. But their environmental evolution within that space may differ significantly: for Asians negative stereotypes are rampant, whereas for Europeans though relevant they are all but totally inconsequential (3). In human genes, as in social science, Asians may have much in common with Europeans, but otherwise descend from a distinct social heritage.

Thus, analysis of commonality in some respects may co-exist with contrasts in others. As pertains to the stereotype of Asian-Americans, Euro-Americans who would presume them the "model minority" would be in error. The most significant consequence of this error has been a subsequent tendency to underestimate the impact of stereotypes because an analogous impact does not pertain to the Euro-American experience i.e.: Eurocentrism. As a result their perceptions of Asian-Americans is less accurate than of other groups because it misses the crux of the Asian existential experience. In the hyper-utilization of "model minority" stereotypes, Asian-Americans are in effect disserved. That disservice is an augmentation of Eurocentrism and is tantamount to the trivialization of Asian people. In the context of social science, trivialization ultimately derives and sustains pathologies among Asian populations who must assimilate into Western societies (4).

Asian-Americans maintain a cultural belief that effort is key in realizing success in higher education (5). This fact differentiates Asian-American mothers from others. Non-Asian-American mothers are of the belief that ability is the key factor in determining the outcome of academic performance. Among Asian-Americans there is the belief that effort is the most important factor in academic success and failure (6). Such a notion is supported in that Asian-American students in higher education report that cultural values play a significant role not only in education but in their personal and interpersonal lives as well.

The personal and interpersonal attributes of Asian-Americans in higher education has been demonstrated by their decreased need for independence as compared to non-Asian-American students (7). When compared to non-Asian-American students Asian-Americans are also more conforming to authority figures (8). They display a greater sense of control over nature and harbor a greater sense of obligation than their Euro-American counterpart (9).

The cultural advantages of Asian-American students in higher education are not without exceptions. Both males and females tend to score significantly below non-Asian-American students on the need for heterosexuality (10). As for impulse expression, Asian-American females in higher education are less prepared than their non Asian-American counterparts to express impulses and to seek gratification either in conscious thought or by overt action (11).

Despite cultural mores, however, Asian-American students were not without sexual experiences (12).

Education is key to the Asian-American stereotype. Scholars of higher education have paid particular attention to the accomplishment of Asian-Americans, which have come to characterize the Asian population in toto. Bankston, Caldas, and Zhou found personality differences in Asian-Americans (13). According to their research, Asian-American males and females appear less oriented than other groups to theoretical and/or abstract ideas, and concepts. Both sexes also dislike uncertainty, ambiguity, and novel, experimental situations, preferring to have more structure.

As it does for other people of color, education has cultural implications for Asian-Americans. The importance of higher education among Asian-Americans is readily apparent in the response of Asian-American parents to their children's education. For instance, most Asian-Americans think that doing well in school is fairly important or very important. Almost all Asian-American parents expect their children to go to college and/or possibly graduate school. Crystal, Chen, Fuligni, Stevenson, Hsu, Ko, Kitamura, and Kitamura further suggest that mothers are willing to invest much personal energy to see to it that their children are well educated (14).

The majority of Asian-American students regard an education as one of the foremost symbols of prestige and success. Their parents, especially those who are first generation and who may have experienced problems in America, prefer that their children major in fields that would bring them the most financial benefit. The overall importance of education to Asian-Americans was established by Chen and Stevenson, who implied that Asian-American families at home and abroad embrace the belief that one should not engage in romance while in school (15). To do so would interfere with academic performance, which is· obviously fundamental to educational success.

Aside from the cultural and personality differences between Asian-Americans and non-Asian-Americans in higher education, findings in the areas of academic abilities and career interests also indicate differences. Kao, Nagata, and Peterson suggest that Asian-American students are less verbal than non-Asian-American groups (16). This would equate with lower scores on tests of verbal abilities and facility.

In other areas of higher education, Asian-American students are more able. Looking at career interests, Chen and Stevenson reported that Asian-Americans had significantly stronger interests in the physical sciences, skilled technical trades, and business detail professions (17). Asian-American males are more interested in the skilled-technical trades and are less interested in sales and verbal-linguistic fields. Thus, most Asian-Americans choose majors in engineering or the physical sciences and are less represented in majors such as sales, social science, and verbal linguistic areas. It can thus be concluded from the aforementioned that culture is significantly related to success in higher education and the Asian-American stereotype as model minority.

There are two alternatives for circumventing Eurocentric stereotypes and correcting this methodological flaw. The first is utilization of the democratic process: incorporating a multiplicity of demographic tools and settling upon the most popular. This approach would prove fitting in a democratic sovereignty but not necessarily effective. Furthermore, demographic tools contingent upon popularity run the risk of collapsing into an intellectual waste that is unproductive and no less hegemonic than Eurocentric stereotypes. The second alternative suggests a more encompassing and universal approach. This approach must accommodate an effort to understand a unique population. As previously mentioned: although Asians and Euro-Americans have a distinct evolutionary heritage, they also have in common both a desire to be accurately portrayed and a disdain for personal stereotypes. Consequently, the termination of stereotypes will prove less Eurocentric and more proximate in a millennium where the diversity of people worldwide is substantial and critical to social science (18).

Eurocentrism in social science is a perspective that has had an impact throughout the history of research on Asians (19). This otherwise obvious assumption is not the least subject to challenge. Social science is no doubt a recapitulation of the present world-system, which has been dominated by a Western geo-political culture since Europe's colonial imperialism. What is more, as part of a geo-political culture, social science originated largely in Europe (20). Thus, until 1945 it was centralized in the West including France, Great Britain, Germany, Italy, and the United States. Furthermore, despite the globalization of knowledge, social science remains a bastion of Eurocentric operatives (21). Commensurate with said operatives, social science evolved in correlation to Eurocentric problems, Eurocentric perspectives, and Eurocentric concepts. Thus, it was virtually inevitable that the ability of Asian-Americans to be depicted accurately would be impacted. That impact reflects the Eurocentric stereotypes of Asians despite the obvious inaccuracy. In the aftermath, scientific institutions have become arguably marketing outlets of Eurocentric perspectives (22). This pronounced contradiction between the ethos of social science and the experiences of an increasingly diverse population has mandated profound challenges to its current structure and ideological configuration. In order to remain viable in a diverse population era, social science must accommodate flexibility in thinking to facilitate emerging trends in population shifts. The inability to do so will encourage accusations of elitism from the very populations social science proposes to serve (23). The unforeseen implication of this elitism is that social science will convert to something myopic in both shape and substance. It will then lend itself increasingly to the auspices and/or influences of Eurocentric standards, i.e.: stereotypes (24). In an effort to succeed, the potential of social scientists will accordingly fall to the pressures of Eurocentric forces. Contesting Eurocentric stereotypes is an effort to accurately portray Asian-American people as they are.

Following WWII and the colonial liberation of Asia and Africa, the consciousness' of non-European people worldwide changed dramatically (25). This had an impact upon social science traditions. In the aftermath of that impact, Eurocentric stereotypes have been subjected to persistent challenges from people of color (26). Those challenges are no doubt fundamentally justified in the efforts of social science to evolve. The script is that social science must challenge stereotypes of Asian-American people, which have dominated the literature (27). The task is no doubt multifaceted and complex. Current population trends will require more accurate depictions to break the hold of Eurocentric stereotypes on the traditions of social science research.

Stereotypes as pertain to Asian-Americans historically have dominated the Western social science literature. According to Lippmann stereotypes are "pictures in our heads" (28). Howard Ehrlich thought of them as "a set of beliefs and disbeliefs about any group of people" (29). The esteemed Gordon Allport insisted that "a stereotype is an exaggerated belief associated with a category" (30). Much like prejudice, definitions of stereotype highlight certain aspects of a people while completely ignoring others. Unfortunately for Asian-Americans what gets highlighted is far from what is accurate.

In reality, the West has relied upon stereotype to call attention to racist beliefs that characterize Asian-Americans inaccurately. What is more, stereotypes vis-à-vis the aforementioned definitions although assumed may not presume the accuracy of fact or even relevancy. Nonetheless, most Westerners apply stereotypes to exaggerations or speculations, which are totally untrue (31). Even the otherwise intelligent and conscientious citizen who would reject stereotypes may firmly believe that they extend from some element of truth.

For purposes of studying Asian-Americans it is assumed that the model minority stereotype is a communal, but unscientifically validated belief about the performances and behaviors of out-group populations, i.e.: Asian. This assumption acknowledges the existence of in-group stereotypes that extend from the same situation. However, in-group stereotypes are not normally as destructive because they are less given to external definition. The primary purpose here is to expose the factless and derogatory stereotypes that Americans and others in the West frequently hold about Asian-Americans as an extension of post-colonial doctrines of racism and superiority. The existence of an Asian-American stereotype in Western folklore suggests that those who subscribe to it are at best ignorant and at worst racist. Its potency is formidable to the extent that Asian-American students who do not live up to exceptional academic standards may succumb to health threatening stressors who are otherwise healthy and normal. Thus, model minority stereotypes may negatively impact Asian-Americans in similar ways that the intellectual inferior stereotypes impact the academic performance of African-Americans.

In modern day America media attention to the model minority intellectual stereotype of Asian-Americans is particularly prevalent in higher education. It drives the stereotype of Asian-American males as weak and unmanly in the revenue-producing sports such as basketball, football, etc. In America the potency of stereotypes is enabled by media technology. Aside from the fact that children are first exposed to racial and ethnic stereotypes primarily in the home and neighborhood, the mass media has extended images of the model minority stereotype beyond comprehension. Hence, on the eve of television technology a well-known study conducted by Berelson and Salter concluded that out-groups were most likely to be presented in stereotyped ways (32). Similar conclusions can be drawn today from movies, magazines, textbooks, and even educational materials!

For purposes of studying Asian-Americans it is assumed that the "model minority" stereotype is a belief, but an unscientifically validated belief about the nature of Asian populations in toto. This assumption acknowledges the existence of in-group stereotypes by Europeans of themselves. However, in-group stereotypes are normally accommodated by the possession of power and are, thus, favorable images that powerful in-groups ordinarily cherish about themselves (33). The primary purpose here is to expose the factless and derogatory stereotypes that the European in-group frequently hold about the Asian out-group as an extension of Eurocentrism. The existence of a "model minority" stereotype suggests that those who subscribe to it are at best ignorant and at worst racist. Thus, persons who would ascribe to "model minority" stereotypes will attribute any non-stereotypical behavior, trait, or talent among Asian-Americans to luck or the influence of European ancestry.

Several Asian groups reside in America, including Vietnamese, Laotian, Hmong and Cambodian (34). While they may appear to be one in the same to many people, they are each a very separate culture, with traditions and history unique to its own members.

The adult Hmong population is likely to be less educated because only a small number of Hmong migrants have had access to schooling since 1960. A written Hmong language was not developed until 1952. Adult Hmong living in the West are likely to be illiterate. Because of this, Hmong people believe strongly in education for their children. They have many cultural differences, which make transition for the Hmong population difficult. For example, in the Hmong culture it is not unusual for boys and girls to marry between the ages of 14 and 18 years (35). For Hmong teens in the West, this practice is not only impractical but illegal as well. Concern for their children is an issue, which worries Hmong parents. They feel it is difficult to raise "good Asian children" obedient, responsible, properly mannered, and willing to abstain from premarital sex in a Western environment. This is an area of great concern to all Asian-American families. Young adults are quickly adopting customs and behaviors of their Western peers. These behaviors are often unacceptable to Asian parents, resulting in a severe generation gap.

Of the four groups, the Vietnamese have had the most direct contact with the West prior to migration. Military efforts in Vietnam from early 1960 to 1973 provided the Vietnamese with an opportunity to know, observe, and form opinions about Americans. Their knowledge of the English language and Western culture helped ease the transition from Vietnam to Western society. The Vietnamese have very strong work and education values. These two traits have been predictors of success and pose no conflict to Western norms.

Family is the central social unit for Laotian people (36). Extended families are common and it is not unusual for several generations to live in one household. Respect and obligations to the family are of extreme importance to Laotians. The majority of them are Buddhists and have integrated their religion into their daily life. Buddhism teaches that a person's behavior in this life will affect the conditions of his/her next life. They tend to be more concerned with personal spiritual development rather than improving social conditions. Their traditional belief suggests that happiness comes from the acceptance of life rather than struggling to change it. One of the issues facing Laotian families similar to the Hmong is the language barrier between generations. Often the parents are not able to speak English and the children are, which causes tension in the family and a breakdown in communication (37).

Crime and violence are increasing at an alarming rate within the Asian refugee communities today (38). The current notion that Asians are overachievers and exceptional students is quickly diminishing as subsequent waves of less educated, rural refugees arrive in America. Education administrators and teachers do not know how to ensure success for these students. Since 1979, many Asian-American youths who emigrated West from Southeast Asian refugee camps have never experienced a classroom in their entire lives. New arrivals as old as 19 are often enrolled in the ninth grade, and must learn to compete with more experienced students. They become increasingly frustrated because they are often unable to measure up to the "model minority" stereotype held by teachers. Some become disciplinary problems, while others drop out of school before completing a full year.

Since 1975, the West has received three major waves of refugees, each having a dramatic impact on the American educational and criminal justice systems. The first wave of refugees arrived immediately following the collapse of the Vietnamese government.

They were the sophisticated, educated, and professional elite who were prepared for a newer life (39). They arrived bearing certain skills and assets that proved later to provide a cushion while they learned how to cope. Their children were expected to excel and they did.

The second wave of refugees to arrive from Southeast Asia were the boat people. This group left Vietnam after the country collapsed and its borders were sealed. At sea, they encountered vicious Thai pirates who often robbed, murdered, kidnapped, or raped them. In many instances, boats were sunk by the pirates or lost in heavy seas.

The third wave of refugees to leave Southeast Asia began in 1979, and consisted primarily of people fleeing from Cambodia. Most of the people in this wave of refugees were uneducated, illiterate and unskilled. The children from this wave were witnesses to unrelenting horror and persecution following the purge of Cambodia, where an estimated three million were killed and hundreds of thousands uprooted from their homes and villages. They arrived suffering severe psychological problems resulting from tremendous physical hardships and mental anguish (40). It is from this wave of refugees that schools began experiencing high numbers of dropouts and other problems involving Asian-American youth. This wave of refugees shattered the "model minority" myth.

Most of the youth who arrived in the first wave of refugees came with intact families. With family support, they quickly learned to speak English. They were forced to attend school, and were expected to excel, because that meant they would get better jobs, therefore the family could survive. As they became successful in school, they became translators for their parents, who often took them out of school to interpret for them at the welfare offices, the clinics, and even at the markets. Today, these youths are caught between two cultures they cannot understand. In the Western classrooms, they are expected by parents to be studious and well disciplined, and by teachers to become more assertive and independent—traits not usually acceptable in the Asian culture (41). As a result, conflict and tensions developed. Many of these youth have become "detached" from their families and their cultures. They see America as a free and promiscuous society where life is better spent in the fast lane. They want to be free of the cultural obligations that bind them to family servitude. Gangs become a welcome relief where they, like the third wave Cambodians, are able to find support and identity.

Most of the youth who arrived in the third wave of refugee resettlement were born and raised in the last days of countries falling apart, others were born in refugee camps. They are characterised by illiteracy even in their own language and culture. They have little or no emotional support system. In America, they find themselves eager to become attached to anything that can provide an escape from the loneliness that has engulfed them. That escape, unfortunately, is often found by becoming attached to fellow outcasts in organized crime.

Asian Organized Crime (AOC) groups are becoming increasingly involved in murder, kidnapping, extortion, gambling, drugs, and money laundering. It has been suggested that AOC has the potential to become the number-one law enforcement problem in America. Amongst the AOC groups that pose as a continuous threat is the Vietnamese Organized Crime. Vietnamese Organized Crime is comprised of Vietnamese immigrants from two distinctive phases. Prior to the fall of Saigon in 1975, the number of immigrants was small. These individuals were older, better educated, and more familiar with the politics and social systems of the West. The second and larger influx of Vietnamese occurred after 1977. As a group, these individuals were younger and less educated. Included in this exodus were many criminals involved in extortion, drug trafficking, prostitution, and gambling. Once these immigrants settled in the West, they proceeded to prey on the established and wealthy Vietnamese from the first group. These young individuals found it easy to extort money through fear and intimidation. They are known for being highly mobile and having family or associates in various parts of the West. This mobility supplies those involved

in criminal activity with convenient hideouts in the homes of un-
suspecting relatives or associates (42).

To many Americans, Asians are stereotyped as overachievers.
They all seem studious, independent, and hard working. Most,
furthermore, believe that Asians have too much pride to ask for
help or assistance. However, the concept of a "model minority" has
caused Asians to retreat into invisible communities where their
many problems are easily overlooked or ignored by governmental
and social service agencies. Problems encountered by law enforcement with regard to investigating AOC are somewhat unique, primarily due to cultural and social factors like language.

Language differences have a tendency to discourage victims or
witnesses from reporting criminal offences or interacting with non-
Asians. As a result of past experiences in their homelands many
Asian-Americans are suspicious of the police, whom they often
view as being corrupt or brutal. Asian-American crime is then more
difficult to investigate and prosecute because Asian-American citizens are reluctant to deal with the criminal justice system. Lack of
understanding resulted in citizens not reporting crime and/or co-
operating with the police. Very little is being done to analyse or
study the causes of Asian-American crime and victimization. Hence,
there has been little success in involving Asian youth in gang prevention and intervention efforts.

The Asian community has perhaps the greatest propensity
toward increased gang activity (43). Asian youth tend to join gangs
for many of the same reasons American youth join gangs. However, because they are a population of different cultural historical
values, recently thrown into the Western milieu, they have many
other relevant issues affecting their families. Of much concern is
the degree of violence and boldness, which is becoming more evident among Asian gangs. Asian gangs are primarily known for
"smash and grab" gun shop robberies. Police report them as being
very bold and exhibiting less fear than juvenile gang youth of other
races. Other criminal activities common to Asian gangs are car
thefts, burglaries and drug sales. Recently, it has become apparent

that Asian groups serve as a connection for other gangs to purchase weapons (44). Furthermore, a very important issue, which must be addressed when dealing with Asian youths, is the degree to which they were exposed to violence, homelessness, and other stresses of war.

Asian-American street gangs are a rapidly growing problem in America. Asian-American youths are victims of language and cultural differences, economic deprivation, racism, social tensions, and limited opportunities. They are marginalized culturally, living "lost" between their families' culture and their target Western culture, and accepted by neither. They are seeking money, recreation, independence, power, protection, identity, and "family." Their arrival into gang life coincided with increasing violence in street life. Guns are readily available to such youths and these youths seem ready to use all weaponry. There is speculation that some Asian-American youth are particularly violent because they witnessed so much violence in their country of origin. While they found life on the streets and in school to be increasingly hostile, gangs provided both power and protection. These gangs are profit driven, violent, young and abusive. Saving face is one of their most important traditions. To lose face is the worst thing that can happen and is often corrected through violent revenge. Asian gang members will then buy the best quality guns because guns symbolize power (45). They wear no "colors" and are not "turf" oriented. Not being turf oriented, it is common for a crime to be perpetrated over 400 miles from where the gang member lives. A gang member will "jump" from one gang to another; they also tend to commit crimes in their own communities.

Asian-American gang members are known to have dealt drugs and committed murder, robbery, burglary, extortion, auto theft, rape, intimidation of witnesses, welfare fraud, and false identification for financial rewards. They are very sophisticated criminals and will learn the habits of their victim. Gang members will sometimes intimidate or assault family members of their intended victim in order to get what they want. There is a large under reporting of these crimes because of past experiences with corrupt officials and people in authority. Perhaps gang members blend into the community where they are more likely to victimize their own people because of fewer language or cultural barriers. They have a negative impact on the lives of the youths involved as well as the community at-large. Thus, gang involvement pertaining to Asian-Americans usually results in criminal activity.

Eurocentric stereotypes of Asian-Americans are unrealistic and born out of racism. Lack of interaction between different social and/or racial groups enable dogma generated from political objective and personal observations. The interpretations of one racial group by another are filtered through local experiences (46). To define Asian-Americans and to derive meaning about Asians based upon European norms and values, without the benefit of legitimate science or personal contact, force conjecture manifested as stereotypes. These stereotypes enable inaccurate depictions and conclusions about the reality of Asian people.

Davis has unveiled the motive for stereotype as a racist preoccupation emanating from fear generated within the Eurocentric status quo (47). He presumes that Euro-Americans anticipate losing economic, political, and educational superiority hence the motive for stereotyping the so-called "model minority." In the past non-Europeans were denied access to competition with Europeans for two reasons: (a) the West practiced segregation; and (b) it was believed that non-European people were inferior to Europeans. Once competition became integrated and non-Europeans began to excel, Europeans rationalized that it was due to abnormal circumstances (48). This notion assured the presumption of the Asian-American stereotype not unrelated to competition in corporate boardrooms and political arenas. In the aftermath the European status quo was assumed secure.

It is the intent of social science to examine the Asian-American "model minority" stereotype in contrast with the evolution of Asian gangs. The evolution of Asian gangs throughout Western societies has been all but ignored due to the Eurocentric hegemony of Western social science literature. By exposing the existence of Asian-American gangs it is hoped that the futility of all manner of stereo-type will be exposed. It is not the intent of social science to deter-mine one race's social superiority over the other. In fact, social science supports the notion that social and cultural variables facili-tated by stereotype significantly impact the social performance of Europeans in the same way that it impacts the social performance of Asian-Americans.

The trepidation and apprehension of Euro-Americans cause them to subjugate Asian-Americans by whatever means necessary—including social science—to maintain a caste system of privilege and opportunity that has operated for decades at the expense of Asian quality of life (49). When Asian-Americans perform at their optimal capacity and Euro-Americans perform at theirs in an envi-ronment unpolluted by racism and stereotype, mankind will ben-efit. In the new millennium it is indeed appropriate to put to rest the pseudo-scientific myths of the "model minority" that disable representation of Asian-Americans by purporting stereotype rather than who they are as a people.

References

(1) Gitterman, A. 1991. Handbook of social work practice with vulnerable populations. New York: Columbia University Press.
(2) Germain, C. 1991. Human Behavior in the Social Envi-ronment: An ecological view. New York: Columbia Univer-sity Press.
(3) Frost, P. 1988. Human skin color: A possible relationship be-tween its sexual dimorphism and its social perception. Per-spectives in Biology and Medicine, 32(1), 38-58.
(4) Arroyo, J. 1996. Psychotherapist bias with Hispanics: An ana-log study. Hispanic Journal of Behavioral Sciences, 18(1), 21-28.

(5) Chen, C., & Stevenson, H. (1995). Motivation and mathematics achievement: A comparative study of Asian-American, Caucasian-American, and East Indian high school students. Child Development, 66(4), 1215-1234.

(6) Ibid

(7) Tomita, S. (1998). The consequences of belonging: Conflict management techniques among Japanese Americans. Journal of Elder Abuse and Neglect, 9(3), 41-68.

(8) Ibid

(9) Geschwender, J. (1992). Ethnicity and the social construction of gender in the Chinese diaspora. Gender & Society, 6(3), 480-507.

(10) Connors, J. (1976). Family bonds, maternal closeness, and the suppression of sexuality in three generations of Japanese Americans. Ethos, 4(2), 189-221.

(11) Ibid

(12) Kulig, J. (1994). Sexuality beliefs among Cambodians: Implications for health care professionals. Health Care for Women International, 15(1), 69-76.

(13) Bankston, C., Caldas, S., & Zhou, M., (1997). The academic achievement of Vietnamese American students: Ethnicity as social capital. Sociological Focus, 30(1), 1-16.

(14) Crystal, D., Chen, C., & Fuligni, A., Stevenson, H., Hsu, C., Ko, H. Kitamura, S. & Kitamura, S. (1994). Psychological maladjustment and academic achievement: A cross-cultural study of Japanese, Chinese, and American High School Students. Child Development, 65(3), 738-753.

(15) Chen, C., & Stevenson, H., (1995). Motivation and mathematics achievement: A comparative study of Asian-American, Caucasian-American, and East Indian high school students. Child Development, 66(4), 1215-1234.

(16) Kao, E. Nagata, D., & Peterson, C., (1997). Explanatory style, family expressiveness and self-esteem among Asian American and European American college students. Journal of Social Psychology, 137(4), 435-444.

(17)) Chen, C. & Stevenson, H. (1995). Motivation and math-
ematics achievement: A comparative study of Asian-American,
Caucasian-American, and East Indian high school students.
Child Development, 66(4), 1215-1234.

(18) Lee, Y. 1991. Stereotypes, silence and threats: The determi-
nants of perceived group homogeneity. Dissertation Abstracts
International, 52(6-B), 3342.

(19) Stinson, A. 1979. Community development in an era of paradigm search. Social Development Issues, 3(3), 6-21.

(20) Hagen, J. 1982. Whatever happened to 43 Elizabeth I? Social Service Review, 56(1), 108-119.

(21) Joyner, C. 1978. The historical status of American Indians
under international law. Indian Historian, 11(4), 30-36, 63.

(22) Schiele, J. 1997. An Afrocentric perspective on social welfare
philosophy and policy. Journal of Sociology and Social Welfare, 24(2), 21-40.

(23) Tambor, M. 1979. The social worker as worker: a union perspective. Administration in Social Work, 3(3), 289-300.

(24) Park, S. & Green, C. 2000. Is transracial adoption in the best
interest of ethnic minority children?: Questions concerning
legal and scientific interpretations of a child's best interests.
Adoption Quarterly, 3(4), 5-34.

(25) Karenga, M. 1995. Making the past meaningful: Kwanza
and the concept of Sankofa. Reflections, 1(4), 36-46.

(26) Ngozi, B. 1997. The Us organization, Maulana Karenga, and
conflict with the Black Panther Party: a critique of sectarian
influences on historical discourse. Journal of Black Studies,
28(2), 157-170.

(27) Potocky, M. & Rodgers-Farmer, A. 1998. Social work research with minority and oppressed population: Methodological issues and innovations. Journal of Social Service Research,
23(3/4), entire issue.

(28) Klineberg, O. 1974. Pictures in our heads, in E. Schuler, T.
Hoult, D. Gibson & W. Brookover, eds. Readings in Sociology, 5th ed. New York: Crowell, 631-637.

(29) Ehrlich, H. 1973. The Sociology of Prejudice. New York: Wiley.

(30) Allport, G. 1958. The Nature of Prejudice. Garden City, NY: Doubleday.

(31) Bogle, D. 1989. Toms, Coons, Mulattoes, Mammies and Bucks: An Interpretive History of Blacks in American Film. New York: Continuum.

(32) Berelson, B. & Salter, P. (1946). Majority and minority Americans: An analysis of magazine fiction. Public Opinion Quaterly, 10, Summer, 168-190.

(33) Charnofsky, H. 1968. Baseball player self conception versus the popular image. International Review of Sport Sociology, 3, 44-46.

(34) Frye, B. 1995. Use of cultural themes in promoting health among Southeast Asian refugees. American Journal of Health Promotion, 9(4), 269-280.

(35) Rogers, J. & Miller, A. 1993. Inner-city birth rates following enactment of the Minnesota Parental Notification Law. Law and Human Behavior, 17(1), 27-42.

(36) Vandiver, V., Jordan, C., Keopraseuth, K., & Yu, M. 1995. Family empowerment and service satisfaction: An exploratory study of Laotian families who care for a family member with mental illness. Psychiatric Rehabilitation Journal, 19(1), 47-54.

(37) Rumbaut, R. 1995. Vietnamese, Laotian and Cambodian Americans. In Asian Americans. Min, P. (Ed.). vol. 174, 232-270.

(38) Westermeyer, J. & Chitasombat, P. 1996. Ethnicity and the course of opiate addiction: Native-born Americans vs. Hmong in Minnesota. American Journal on Addictions, 5(3), 231-240.

(39) Bankston, C. 1998. Sibling cooperation and scholastic performance among Vietnamese-American secondary school students: An ethnic social relations theory. Sociological Perspectives, 41(1), 167-184.

(40) Chow, L. 1995. Depression and anxiety among Cambodian, Laotian, and Vietnamese refugees. Dissertation Abstracts, 56(6-B).

(41) Rousseau, C. & Drapeau, A. 2000. Scholastic achievement of adolescent refugees from Cambodia and Central America. Adolescence, 35(138), 243-258.

(42) Jan, L. 1993. Asian gang problems and social policy solutions. Journal of Gang Research, 1(4), 37-44.

(43) Joe, K. 1994. The new criminal conspiracy? Asian gangs and organized crime in San Francisco. Journal of Research in Crime and Delinquency, 31(4), 390-415.

(44) Kwok, J. 1990. Advisor, emergency immigration education assistance program & Los Angeles Police Department Asian gang task force.

(45) Ibid

(46) Kitano, H. (1997). Race Relations. 5th ed. Upper Saddle River, NJ: Prentice-Hall.

(47) Davis, L. 1991. The Articulation of Difference: White Preoccupation with the Question of Racially Linked Genetic Differences Among Athletes. Sociology of Sport Journal, 7(2), 179-187.

(48) Hunter, D. 1998. Race and athletic performance: A physiological review in African Americans in Sport ed. G. Sailes, 85-101, New Brunswick: Transaction.

(49) Kitano, H. 1997. Race Relations. 5th ed. Upper Saddle River, NJ: Prentice-Hall.

IX

Eurasian Identity

The stigmatization of dark skin has been an American controversey for quite some time. Many are of the opinion that it is simply an ugly chapter in American history. Asian-Americans, on the other hand, are forced to live with the consequences of their skin color in every waking moment of their lives. It should then come as no surprise that skin color has caused some internal strife. Much of this strife has impacted identity. Being dark-skinned in a culture where skin color is threatening, people of color began to define themselves negatively (1). If there were less variation in color it might be less of a problem, but given the circumstances of history, people of color have not experienced opportunity equally (2). As they put pressure on the American political structure to dismantle obstacles to success, those in a position to take advantage in greatest numbers have been those with the lightest skin (3). This in and of itself is not necessarily a problem, but there are codes of behavior and a history associated with it.

Germane to the racist concept of the black/white dichotomy is skin color. As pertains to identity, racism is the belief that superiority is racially based in every respect and any deviations from it—including identity models—are inferior, attaching a stigma to any non-European characteristic, i.e. dark skin. The general assumptions underlying this analysis are as follows: (a) concepts of identity are rooted in a socio-political context, although it is seldom articulated; (b) that assumption in America is acted out including racism among people of color in the example of marital patterns; (c) a competing model of identity based on human development across the lifespan challenges the racist taint of the black/white dichotomy; (d) such a model is grist for legitimate research that may be useful in the objective analyses of a Eurasian identity; and (e) this alternative model empowers Eurasian-Americans by offering an option to the traditional race rhetoric (4).

Traditional models of identity then stress the importance of racial characteristics like skin color. As per such models, identity development progresses toward a specific predetermined end-state (5). Its role is twofold: initially race, is to emotionally sustain and, secondly, to serve as a psychological reference point (6). On the basis of race and racial characteristics, traditional models determine how the dynamics of identity development are comprehended. Dominated by racial canons the process is assumed to be complete at a particular point in physiological development regardless of culture, class, or social experience. Identity under the circumstances is static and manifests prior to adulthood. Such a view has dominated the post-colonial era and its institutions reflecting a philosophical perspective that reinforces certain schools of thought that accommodate racial thinking. The result is tantamount to hegemony and validates models commensurate with the black/white dichotomy otherwise lacking in scholarly merit. Significant advancement in media such as film and other video technologies then profoundly extends the influence of those who advocate race as the definitive identity element couched in the African-American "tragic mulatto." Extended from that theme is the biracial beginning of the Eurasian identity experience in America.

The potency of Eurasian identity can be assessed in post-colonial video technology. The "tragic mulatto" represented biracial African-Americans born into a world that defined them as African-American by any trace of African heritage. Donald Bogle, in a well researched effort, offers a detailed chronology beginning with a film called "The Debt," released in 1912 (7). Set in the old South, a white man's wife and his black mistress bear him children simultaneously. After growing up together, the white son and the biracial daughter become romantically involved with one another and decide to get married. Eventually, it is revealed to them at the crucial moment that they are in fact brother and sister. Their lives are thus ruined not only because they are kin but also because the girl has black blood. The white skin and blue eyes that would otherwise define her as white are irrelevant, rendering her societal identification as black.

In reality many post-colonial biracial African-Americans left the South for the North where they could pass for white. "Pinky," another film released in 1949, features a biracial nurse who returns to the South, having passed for white in the North. She is depressed by the Southern life of daily threats and insults. Pinky plans to return North to her white fiancée and her life as a white woman in a free society. But her black grandmother convinces her to stay with her people. She confides to her white fiancée in the North: "Tom, you can change your name. . . . I'm a Negro. I can't deny it. . . ." And so, as was true of all biracial African-Americans, Pinky's life meets tragedy by way of the traditional standards of racial identity.

In real life Dorothy Dandridge exemplified the ultimate metaphor of "tragic mulatto" in the failings of her film career. Her life and stardom were reported by the white and black presses. The biracial attributes, which may have enabled her professionally, may have forced her to live out a screen image that eventually destroyed her. *Carmen Jones* was the celebrated film that established her as the definitive "tragic mulatto." In it her love interest was a "good colored boy" portrayed by Harry Belafonte. Carmen convinces him to desert the army, after which they end up in a Chicago hotel. She then leaves him for a prize fighter, and is later strangled by him for her unfaithfulness. Subsequently Dandridge appeared to bring the tragedy of her biracial identity to her film characters. And in fact, for Dandridge, on screen and off, the tragedy of real life was in her being biracial.

The remainder of Dandridge's film career was an authentic account of the "tragic mulatto." Regardless of talent, film studios were unable to think of her in any terms but as the exotic, doomed mulatto, caught between two worlds by the limitations of race. Plans were discussed for starring her in Cleopatra, but were eventually discarded. The tragedy of her life lives on to this day. Rumors and stories circulate about her retarded daughter, her "hidden" son, her white father, and of her white lovers. She was reportedly involved with everyone in Hollywood from Tyrone Power to Peter Lawford. Such rumors perhaps enabled Dandridge to bring integrated love scenes to American film by making "Island in the Sun." But due to its theme of miscegenation, "Island in the Sun" was marred by controversy. Prior to its release Southern theaters threatened to boycott it. The South Carolina state legislature began preparations to pass a bill that would penalize any movie house $5000 that showed the film. In consequence of her biracial identity, Dorothy Dandridge fled the United States in hopes of film success in Europe. There she was allowed to star opposite white love interests, but because of the interracial love theme no major American company would distribute her work, which led ultimately to failure. Rumor has it she succumbed to alcoholism, drugs, and destructive love affairs. Finally, in 1965, at the age of forty-one, Dorothy Dandridge was found dead, the victim of an overdose of anti-depression pills. The tragedy of Dandridge's life is that, as a biracial person, racial models of identity denied her the possibility of fulfillment either as completely black or completely white. Identity for biracial African-Americans was no less tragic for men than for women. It dominated the lives of common folk.

Themes of the "tragic mulatto" among men were equally convincing via their portrayal in literature. In Walter White's (8) "A Man Called White" the oppressions of racial identity models are revealed through chance encounter and coincidence. While waiting for a train in New York City, Mr. White stepped on the toe of a darker-skinned black man standing behind him. He turned to apologize to find the man starring at him. The man's face was hard and full of the piled-up bitterness of racism and lynching (9). The man shouted obscenities and asked Mr. White to look where he was going, accusing white people of always stepping on black people. A moment later Mr. White was approached by another African-American about his work for the NAACP regarding legislation of a permanent Fair Employment Practices Committee. The man whose toe had been stepped on listened then apologized. He had realized that what he thought was a white man was, in fact, Mr. Walter White, leader of the NAACP. Mr. White is not white. He insists there is nothing in his mind or heart that tempts him to think he is. Yet, he realizes that the only attribute of identity that matters in America is the appearance of whiteness. As a biracial man he concedes there is magic in a white skin; there is tragedy, loneliness, and exile in a black skin. He is confused by the lack of logic in that he insists he is black, when nothing compels him to do so but himself.

Finally, Hall in "The Complexion Connection" gives an account of what it is like for biracial African-American men who pass (10). His character insists that, in the cold calculation of a cost-benefit analysis, to want to be black in America is crazy. Once a black person realizes what is denied him based upon the skin color of his relatives—how he is perceived in the minds not only of bad people but of many people who are fundamentally good—his sense of unfairness may overcome him to the extent that he simply cannot accept that part of himself that has been defined as ugly and inferior by race category. He contends that if such a person has no particular political agenda or ethnic loyalty, passing may seem to be a perfectly logical way of getting what he knows he deserves, much as any other American. But being identified as black in America cannot be reduced to an equation or to perfect logic. To live with a decision to pass, many biracial men choose professions that offer them ways to benefit blacks in general—such as law, medicine, and the ministry. In the process they are better able to sustain the psychological pain assuming that their passing as white is to the benefit of black people. Otherwise passing inflicts psychological trauma on those who try it, because it requires them to erect a wall between who they are or could be as persons and who they are or try to be amid white society. Sociologist W.E.B. Du Bois referred to this as double consciousness, a condition that is rooted in racism and is the basis of the mulatto, i.e.: biracial hypothesis.

The "mulatto hypothesis" was put forth by early Euro-American social scientists. They used it to explain away the African-American individuals who excelled intellectually in business or the sciences. This hypothesis further reinforced the belief that light skin was superior to dark. One result was that certain jobs were once routinely given or denied African-Americans based upon their lightness of skin. For example, civil service jobs were highly sought by African-Americans early in the twentieth century. In Chicago, the Euro-American officials responsible for filling those positions felt that an African-American with light skin would fit better into an office populated mostly by Euro-Americans. Also, the menial elevator-operator jobs in the large downtown department stores of northern cities were once reserved for "light-skinned colored girls." Even the African-American community, to its simultaneous shame, fame, and economic enrichment, was home to any number of establishments that were owned and operated by African-Americans but refused to serve the African-American public. In Tulsa, Oklahoma, there was a black-owned, black-operated barbecue cafe that for years did not allow African-Americans to eat at its tables. If you were not light enough to pass, the best you could expect was a plate handed out the back door.

One of the cruelest manifestations of color discrimination in the African-American community was the "brown paper bag test." The result of this color-comparison test was that dark skin was taxed and light skin was awarded status. For example, a campus fraternity or sorority at one of the black colleges would have a party and charge an admission. Anyone with dark skin who attended would incur an additional tax. Light-skinned guests, usually females, would be admitted free. On those same campuses, a dark-skinned black woman could not have been selected as homecoming queen until the 1960s. Euro-Americans must have found such behavior a bit peculiar. For light-skinned blacks, it added yet another reason to disassociate themselves from the African-American community and pass.

There are, in fact, many rationales for passing, some of them fascinating. Most Americans tend to think that passing is an outdated concept relevant only to a distant and ugly past, when dark-skinned people could be lynched with no outcry from the public; Ms. Mary Walker's case dispels that notion. She grew up during the 1960s, at the height of the black pride movement, but was raised in an all-white neighborhood of Denver, Colorado. There her parents—both black—required her and her twelve siblings to pass as white from birth. According to Ms. Walker, her parents believed that life would be better for them if they did not reveal that they were black. The whole family thus had to guard their secret very carefully: the children were reprimanded if they did not straighten their hair on schedule, or if they used black slang.

Mary Walker was not particularly bothered by these restrictions until she went off to a small college in the West where her white cultural norms made her an outcast among African-Americans when she tried to join the Black Student Union on campus. She was told that she was "too white." It was then that she realized that her parents' enforcement of white norms had cost her a major part of her identity. Having no idea what to do about the problem, she decided to ignore it and put her energies into getting her degree.

After graduation, Ms. Walker continued to pass until she was in her thirties, when she decided to advocate the hiring of more black teachers at the school where she was employed, and in so doing "came out of the closet" about her own passing. Not too surprisingly, the school administration then accused her of trying to take advantage of Affirmative Action policies by suddenly declaring herself to be black when she obviously was not. She claims to have been fired from her job as a result, an irony that generated media interest in her story.

Mary Walker's family may in fact have been more white than

black. A Jew who has one drop of Italian blood is not necessarily Italian. A German who has one drop of French blood is not necessarily French. In fact, no other ethnic group is subjected to the one-drop theory like African-Americans. This essential fact makes the point that to be black is to be subjected to the severest modes of discrimination in America. No white person—much less a light-skinned black or other person of color—would ever want to be subjected to that discrimination.

Any portion of African ancestry is enough to identify one as black, a person must be able to prove at least one-eighth Native American ancestry if they want to claim that as their legal identity. Is it possible that economics has anything to do with it? A black person not only does not have the haven of a reservation, but on the basis of skin color becomes a financial and social outcast as well. Thus, while not a few whites will state with some romantic notion they are "part Indian," none would make reference to their black ancestry. In his autobiography, Malcolm X mentions how he used this aversion to exploit Euro-Americans in the prison system. He would threaten to "expose" them as light-skinned blacks passing for white if they did not do what he asked. To Malcolm, his success with this ploy was obvious proof of what whites thought of black people: They would do anything to avoid being identified as such.

While passing remains a strategy in the African-American community, it has not become any less painful. Numerous examples in literature make that point. Novelists in particular during the 1930s and 1940s have used passing as a theme, though it has been identified more often with full-scale realism than with fiction. Rudolph Fisher, who wrote "Wall of Jericho," reflects this in his work. Walter White's "Flight" and Nella Larson's "Passing," among others, deal with the issue of passing and the pain it causes for light-skinned blacks. But of all the novels treating passing, perhaps the most successful and the most popular is "The Autobiography of an Ex-Colored Man." The popularity of this novel brought passing into the light of discussion. It focused on the "tragic mulatto," unable to fit into either black or white society. The main character—a light-skinned black man—dreams of becoming a composer. But after seeing a mob of whites in the South set fire to a black man, he gives up his ambition to create music. To escape the dangers of being black in America, the character decides to pass as a white businessman. For awhile he is successful, but ultimately he comes to hate himself and winds up tormented by ambivalence toward his identity, morals, and family ties. This novel captures the essence of the trauma experienced by light-skinned blacks who cannot find the strength to endure the stigma associated with their ancestry.

In earlier years, the threat of lynching and other overt practices of racism made passing a much more dangerous undertaking than it is today. For this reason it had evolved into various forms, the most common of which were temporary and permanent. Temporary passing was usually done for practical reasons such as getting a job, etc. Those who passed permanently did so for life, severing all family ties. According to research, the area of the country where a black person lived had much to do with the form of passing he or she practiced. In the North, where whites tended to be more urban and less violent, blacks could pass temporarily. Those with light enough skin would work by day in the cities, where they could carry on as a white person. Since there was so much movement, a person's background often went unknown. This enabled many light-skinned black males to support families. In particular, those who were born in the South and educated as doctors or lawyers could increase their opportunities by passing in the cities "up north."

In the largely rural South, employment opportunities for African-Americans were scarce. The best even a doctor or lawyer could hope for was to work in the black community, and that was possible only if no Euro-American wanted the business. Consequently, passing did offer some possibilities for improving one's station. But in the South, the consequences of being discovered could be life-threatening: Light-skinned black persons passing in the South might well be lynched for impersonating a white. The communities there tended to be much more familiar and associated with one another. Thus, if a black were to pass, the decision would have to be made at birth, by the parents. Even then, moving to a new location was the only way they could keep the ploy intact.

Light-skinned men had a much easier time with passing than women. Their greater mobility provided them with more successes. They might settle in a small town for work, take a white bride, and, with no one suspecting, disappear forever into the white masses. Of course, this required complete disassociation from their families, who might reveal their history. It is hard to imagine what this must have done emotionally to both the families and those who passed. It was, however, the most likely way in America that "black" blood found its way into "white" veins.

Light-skinned black women had a different experience with passing. They were less likely to engage in any form of passing that required a complete dissociation from their backgrounds, since their reputations would suffer in any community where their past could not be traced. They would be morally marked and could never expect to marry into a respectable white family. Also, light-skinned black women had advantages by staying within the black community: Their features made them highly prized as mates—particularly in the middle class, where light skin was a status symbol. Thus, with little regard for morality, talent or character, an attractive, light-skinned black woman might have immediate access to some measure of wealth through marriage to a middle class black man. Such advantages have produced a haughty attitude in a few light-skinned black women that, unfairly, is sometimes assumed to be present in all. Jealousies, also unfair, have erupted among darker-skinned black women around this issue.

Without regard to light skin, traces of African blood necessitates one's identity as black (11). It is the most potent and salient feature because it contrasts with the Western ideal (12). African blood may have an effect upon every phase of life including self-concept and most importantly, identity (13). It is a "master status," which differentiates the race category of Africans from the mainstream as an inferior element of society. So potent is this "master status" that it has recently served as grounds for litigation between persons of light and dark skin color but who belong to the same race group (14). A resort to legal tactics is an indication that for some, identity development has been particularly painful given the psychologically conflicting implications of race. That is, biracial African-Americans have idealized much of Western culture, but unlike members of the mainstream are prohibited from structural assimilation into it (15). Regardless, their willingness to assimilate reflects a desire not to devalue themselves but to improve their quality of life and live the "American Dream." In so doing, they may develop a racist disdain for dark skin because the disdain is an aspect of Western culture (16). They are cognizant of the fact that African blood is regarded by the various Western institutions as an obstacle that might otherwise allow them the opportunities necessary to succeed. For those who labor, unaware of the inherent limitations, failure is the end result. Furthermore, since quality of life closely correlates with having a color approximate to the racial mainstream, light skin has emerged as critical to one's ability to prosper (17).

For those who are biracial in America, this requires/enables living a life of multiple identities (18). At the very least, they evolve in the context of a social universe that demands strict adherence to certain race based norms (19). Alternatively, today's less overt and more covert racism facilitates a separate identity, necessitating its own set of criteria. As a result being biracial then requires two processes. On the one hand, it may precipitate a conscious distancing from the stigmatized race category. On the other hand, it may involve the creation of a new identity based in part upon an inability to be accepted without reservation by Euro and/or African-Americans. That inability demands identity diffusion in the traditional Eriksonian sense; at the same time, a biracial life may exemplify the functional identity of a "black" or "white" American (20). Dependent upon skin color, identity is in fact fluid. Histori-

cally, biracial heritage connoted the actuality of the "tragic mulatto," but this surely has changed. For the first time in modern
day history having "black blood," however little, does not predetermine one's identity as solely "black." But, deserting the racial
canons of identity may mean correcting others in that one is biracial. The process begins with the very first encounter where a biracial person challenges race rhetoric and continues throughout life,
decreasing only to the extent that they are consistently identified
with other than their assigned race category.

The need of biracial Americans for a separate identity contrasts with the degree to which race remains imperative. While
numbers may be few, those who prefer to distance themselves from
their racial heritage must—for mental health reasons—have the
option to do so. This contrast highlights the power of achieved
identity as a cultural concept that is to be developed preceding
adulthood. But for biracial Americans, racist imperatives are unyielding, rendering other than race based identities questionable.
The race dynamic is possible because the biracial identity is removed from its historical and political context. As a result, biracial
lives are assumed unrelated and unresponsive to social circumstances, history, or culture. This allows for the idealization of race
in mythic proportion conveyed by Western culture and its belief
systems (21). The construction of an essentially racial identity then
inhibits fluidity and models that incorporate development across
the lifespan. Models of identity that emerge are inculcated by
pseudo-scholars who perpetuate hegemony, resulting in the many
layers of victimization that post-colonial Eurasian-Americans frequently endure.

Because light-skinned ethnic groups considered themselves
superior to dark-skinned groups, and because light-skinned people
of color were more likely their off-spring, i.e. Eurasian, they were
acceptable long before it was considered possible for the dark-
skinned masses. With each generation acceptance become an ex-
pectation rather than a goal. This meant that light-skinned Eurasian-Americans like African-American mulattoes were able to en-

gage in the most prestigious occupations that ultimately brought them the highest incomes and frequently the resentment of others (22). Not only darker Asian-Americans but poor Euro-Americans resented their success. While it is true that every light-skinned Eurasian-American who succeeded worked hard, it is also true that their light skin facilitated their efforts. This is not the fault of Eurasian-Americans. It is simply the environment in which they evolved. It is that environment that has made their identity development unique.

Historically, Eurasian heritage connoted the actuality of the "tragic mulatto," but this surely has changed. For the first time in modern day history having mixed blood, the "one drop theory"— however little, does not predetermine one's identity. However, deserting the race paradigm may mean correcting others in that one is Eurasian. The process begins with the very first encounter where a Eurasian challenges race rhetoric and continues throughout life, decreasing only to the extent that one is consistently identified with other than the assigned racial category. The pervasiveness of such racism ultimately requires the construction of mechanisms to encompass the unique dynamics of Eurasian identity development.

Not only is Eurasian identity development unique, it is frequently conditioned by ridicule. In early childhood, Eurasians learn that circumstances can be problematic. Comments of disapproval are routine among peers. In contrast to persons who are unmistakably identified by their skin color, Eurasians have grown up inculcating an anti-white rhetoric before they conclude that it is directed at some aspect of their racial heritage. By the time they become of age Eurasians may then be conflicted by identity (23/ 24). Given the stigma associated with dark skin, the ambitious confront major decisions pertaining to where they are going and how to get there. In a racist milieu that affects them personally, they must prioritize American values, standards, and ideals (25). The bright and talented cannot possibly ignore the inherent contradictions between those values, standards, ideals, and their personal lives. For the middle class, who may have been sheltered from such a reality, there are stinging consequences by the time they reach adolescence (26).

Where Eurasians once personified a moral failure as the "illegitimate" off-spring of a post-colonial class, they have today become a national dilemma with considerable social and political implications. For such persons inculcating racist stigmas at an early age is unusually resistant to change (27). Eurasians—like all Americans—have been socialized in the normalcy of a racial identity and have been acculturated to reject stigmatized Asian characteristics, especially those involving stereotypes (28). Becoming conscious of the pervasiveness of racism is difficult, since it demands an awareness of the historical nature of personal identity and an appreciation of the arbitrariness of identity models. Ultimately, as Eurasians acknowledge the motives of racism, the introjected stigmas and stereotypes that have silently directed their lives become clearer. The disentangling of race models from personal history and individual characteristics is an enormously difficult emotional task (29). For this reason, the process of creating identity out of a Eurasian status will be a prolonged and complex undertaking. Exiting from the race model that has been etched into consciousness since birth is profoundly unsettling and is greatly complicated by the many real societal barriers. The task is difficult because the view of the black/white dichotomy is that identity is not considered socially constructed but is rather a static consequence of race (30). No self-consciousness exists about Eurasians—unless one deviates from the universally accepted racial norm. The cultural script is that all Americans must become amenable to a non-racial identity as the nation—and indeed the world—moves toward increased levels of amalgamation.

Work is perhaps the most important decision confronting adolescents regardless of race and/or skin color (31). It will in fact determine their quality of life. As Eurasians mature, contradictions become even more apparent. Equality of opportunity for all Americans has only recently become a societal goal (32). Eurasian

youth observe the prevailing racism in the high rates of employment discrimination. They concur that hard work for them may
not result in the realization of career objectives. Those who aspire
must decide whether or not they will invest their time and energies developing competencies around an identity, because of which,
society may not allow them to fully evolve. The decision to pursue
a particular line of work is then contingent upon risk. For Eurasians, the risk incurred by embracing a stigmatized identity involves their emotional well-being. If they invest themselves totally
in the effort and the effort does not pay off; if they see that equality
in the job market has eluded them in the process; they will face a
profound devastation and lose all respect for societal institutions
(33). Asian-American communities are rife with casualties of previous generations, which consist of talented folk like themselves
who harbored lofty aspirations but reached little more than the
status gained via limitation. The alternative to taking risks—particularly if one is a light-skinned Eurasian—is to distance one's
self from the Asian-American community. Embracing mainstream
society via passing for Euro-American or the creation of a new
identity under the circumstances are both seemingly viable alternatives.

   The need of Eurasians for a separate identity contrasts with the
degree to which race remains a cultural imperative. While numbers
may be few, those who prefer to distance themselves from their Asian
heritage might very well do so. This contrast highlights the power of
achieved identity as a cultural concept that is to be developed preceding adulthood. But for Eurasians, racist imperatives are unyielding,
rendering other than race based identities questionable. This tenacious
distinction reinforces the psychological potency of racism—a socio-political factionalizing of the population via variations in skin color. The
entire dynamic is possible because contemporary identity is removed
from its historical and political context. As a result, Eurasian lives are
assumed unrelated and unresponsive to social circumstances, history,
or culture. This allows for the idealization of race in mythic proportion
conveyed by cultural prescription (34). The construction of an essen-

tially racial identity then inhibits fluidity of human development across the lifespan. Narrow models that emerge are indoctrinated by pseudo-scholars who perpetuate hegemony, resulting in the many layers of victimization that Eurasians frequently endure.

In the interest of mental and emotional health, Asians who perceive themselves as Eurasian must counter-define the social and political universe. In the face of two powerful barriers, racism and psychological domination, it characterizes the viability of their existence. Scholars of cultural diversity stress the process of self-acknowledgment and the proclamation of existence as the first critical step in personal and, later, social acceptance of what is different (35). For Eurasians, this simple proclamation is a revolutionary act in its repudiation of a culturally imposed stigma. They are unique in that their defining difference on the basis of skin color may be non-definitive. Since they can literally choose their identity, via straddling racial categories, the affirmation of identity may be complicated for otherwise absurd racial reasons. Thus, to the degree that identity is actually a socially constructed phenomenon, Eurasians develop their identities under a unique set of circumstances (36). Consolidation of it is more impacted by ambiguity with few positive and many negative consequences. The characteristic ambiguity of "passing-for-white" is nearly always one of difficult consideration. But it is a necessity of slowly and painfully appreciating an identity wholeness that cannot be understood via routine identity developmental models.

The black/white dichotomy is disabled without the traditional race model hypothesis. Pursuit to an alternative explanation is the idea that identity is a fluid social construction that extends across the lifespan of human development (37). In this view, identity is no more static than any other social entity, i.e.: custom, class, or cultural experience. Advocated as a model, the idea that identity is shaped by social circumstances is radical and politically charged. In fact, identity is subject to change and is a malleable component of the social universe. Contrasting models expose the perception of traditional models as thinly veiled manifestations of racism. As per the classic literature, Cooley likened identity development to the "looking glass self." The "looking glass self" is a metaphor that characterizes identity as a reflection of the self in public perception. From that perception the core of identity is fashioned. A similar analysis was proposed by Mead, who contends that identity is a product of social interaction. The process is complete once the subject—one in the process of identity development—has moved from the "I" to the "me" perception of self. Complimenting the work of Mead, Nobles and Cross extended the concept of "I" and "me" to group memberships (38, 39). According to Nobles, group membership bestows a "weness" to the identity development process. Lastly, Erikson initially contended that identity is not static. Vis-à-vis given characteristics it evolves out of a complex of decision-making experiences such as mate selection and lifestyle, which may evolve continuously. Exemplifying the traditional, Erikson later wrote that final identity is fixed "at the end of adolescence." The self as evolution of social experience is well demonstrated in an analysis of Eurasians whose skin color is associated with more than one racial category (40). Enlightened conclusions offer skin color and the development of a Eurasian identity model to point out how traditional models have become obsolete and/or function to reinforce various social and political objectives.

Antithetical to the black/white dichotomy is coming to an appreciation of the cultural myths pertaining to race vis-à-vis skin color. Some of these myths are the obvious negative stereotypes about the associations of dark skin with inferiority and the superiority of European ancestry (41). Others are less well articulated, maintaining that some among Eurasians—particularly the light-skinned—being off-springs of the post-colonial class are arrogant and/or self-centered (42). To the degree that these views have been consciously incorporated, they are easy to challenge, but they must be challenged by demythologizing personal contact. Such occurrences as recognizing other aspects of identity will slowly modify the more deeply entrenched assumptions.

As per the black/white dichotomy, scholars, theorists, and researchers have historically promoted a static unidimensional perspective of identity (43). For example, the view that Eurasian is a non-identity dismisses social factors that shape the manifestation or denial of Eurasian issues. Such analyses readily preclude therapeutic methods designed to alter the assumed deviant identity and social policies/laws that institutionalize the stigmatization of dark skin (44). In contrast, the Eurasian identity must be described using a conceptual model that explicates the complex factors influencing identity development of people in a context over historical time. The most effective model for these processes is a human development across the lifespan perspective (45). This general view, which has many individual variants, involves the explication of patterns of dynamic interaction of multiple factors over time in the development of an individual person. The Eurasian-American must be understood in context; simultaneous descriptions of their social network, neighborhood and community, institutional settings, and culture. These aspects are complemented by descriptions of physical and psychological characteristics. In contrast with earlier views, the lifespan human development model stresses the impact of historical events on the processes of personal identity, whether the processes are observed during an individual's lifespan, over the lifespan of family members, within a community, or in a culture. The lifespan human development model is also an effort to encompass skin color variations among individuals as they move in time through social/political situations, the community, culture, and history. Moreover, Eurasians are not passive recipients of history but have potential to shape circumstances and contexts as well (46).

The lifespan human development model serves as a powerful alternative to the pathologizing influences of the black/white dichotomy and to approaches emphasizing racial characteristics to the exclusion of others. It suggests a very different model from the traditional view. This set of concerns involves personal and social recognition that one's race and/or skin color is not wholly definitive. Generally, this includes understanding the nature of personal preferences and valuing them despite of their existence within a stigmatizing social universe. Initially, the breadth of meaning for the new identity may be uncertain: it may also mean a new perception of the Eurasian self. The stabilization of mental health requires its utilization as an option for desiring Eurasian-Americans.

Evolution of the lifespan human development model complies with the genesis of a new awareness in the behavioral sciences. It is increasingly evident pertinent to the study of identity, self-image, family dynamics, etc. It is a necessity in a nation fastly becoming not only racially but also ethnically and culturally diverse as well. The recent trend of diversity in higher education has facilitated assertions on the part of people of color to define identity for themselves. Their findings have validated the importance of social experience as having a direct correlation to mental health. This has implications for the mental health of Eurasians whose social experience does not conform to the black/white dichotomy. For those who choose the option to define themselves, rather than be defined by superficial racial characteristics, will help sustain society in toto. The evolution of this perspective will encompass and/or facilitate the nation's increasing amalgamation. In its aftermath will prevail the antithesis of the black/white dichotomy. Its legacy will be a redefinition of identity in a more rational apolitical context. For Eurasians, identity models will then be constructed less on the basis of what race they are—vis-à-vis skin color—and more on the basis of who they are—vis-à-vis experience—extended across the lifespan.

References

(1) Hall, R. E. (1992). Bias among African-Americans regarding skin color: Implications for social work practice. Research on Social Work Practice, 2, 479-486.

(2) Washington, R. (1990). Brown Racism and the Formation of a World System of Racial Stratification. International Journal of Politics, Culture, and Society, 4(2), 209-227.

(3) Hughes, M. & Hertel, B. (1990). The significance of color remains: A study of life chances, mate selection, and ethnic consciousness among Black Americans. Social Forces, 68(4), 1105-1120.

(4) Martinez, E. (1993). Beyond Black/White: The racisms of our time. Social Justice, 20, 1-2(51-52), 22-34.

(5) Rivera-Santiago, A. (1996). Understanding Latino ethnic identity development: A review of relevant issues. New England Journal of Public Policy, 11(2), pp. 13-24.

(6) Goldstein, B. (1995). Image and Identity: Mixed Parentage Conference Report. EYTARN.

(7) Bogle, D. (1991). Tom, Coon, Mulattoes, Mammies & Bucks. New York, Continuum Pub.

(8) Hall, R. E. (February, 1995). Blacks who pass. In Herb Boyd and Robert Allen (Eds.). Brotherman: The Odyssey of Black Men in America—An Anthology. Ballantine Books.

(9) Soule, S. (1992). Populism and Black lynching in Georgia. Social Forces, 71(2), pp. 431-449.

(10) Hall, R. E. (February, 1995). Blacks who pass. In Herb Boyd and Robert Allen (Eds.). Brotherman: The Odyssey of Black Men in America—An Anthology. Ballantine Books.

(11) Kitano, H. (1997). Race Relations. New Jersey, Prentice-Hall. Lancaster, R. (1991). Skin color race and racism in Nicaragua. Ethnology, 30(4), 39-353.

(12) Hall, R. E. (1990). The projected manifestations of aspiration, personal values, and environmental assessment cognates of cutaneo-chroma (skin color) for a selected population of African Americans (Doctoral dissertation, Atlanta University, 1989). Dissertation Abstracts International, 50, 3363A.

(13) Owusu, B. (1994). Race, self identity and social work. British Journal of Social Work, 24(2), 123-136.

(14) Hiskey, M. (1990, May 4). Woman sues SCLC, cites skin color bias. The Atlanta Journal Constitution, Sec B, P 5, Col 1.

(15) Kitano, H. (1997). Race Relations. New Jersey, Prentice-Hall. Lancaster, R. (1991). Skin color race and racism in Nicaragua. Ethnology, 30(4), 39-353.

(16) Anderson, L. (1991). Acculturative stress: A theory of relevance to Black Americans.
Clinical Psychology Review. Vol 11(6). 685 702.

(17) Hughes, M. & Hertel, B. (1990). The significance of color remains: A study of life chances, mate selection, and ethnic consciousness among Black Americans. Social Forces, 68(4), 1105-1120.

(18) Richards, W. (1995). Working with "mixed race" young people. Youth and Policy, 49, pp.62-72.

(19) Twine, F. (1996). Brown skinned white girls: Class, culture and construction of white identity in suburban communities. Gender, Place and Culture, 3(2), 205-224.

(20) Bowles, D. (1993). Bi-racial identity: Children born to African American and White couples. Clinical Social Work Journal, 21(4), 417-428.

(21) Hall, R. E. (1993). Clowns, buffoons, and gladiators: Media portrayals of African-American men. The Journal of Men's Studies,1, 239-251.

(22) Mullins, E. & Sites, P. (1990). The contribution of Black women to Black upper class maintenance and achievement. Sociological Spectrum, 10(2), 187-208.

(23) Herring, R. (1995). Developing Eurasian ethnic identity: A review of the increasing dilemma. Journal of Multicultural Counseling and Development, 23(1), 29-38.

(24) Richards, W. (1995). Working with "mixed race" young people. Youth and Policy, 49, pp.62-72.

(25) Hall, R. E. (1993). Clowns, buffoons, and gladiators: Media portrayals of African-American men. The Journal of Men's Studies,1, 239-251.

(26) Bowles, D. (1993). Bi-racial identity: Children born to African American and White couples. Clinical Social Work Journal, 21(4), 417-428.

(27) Falkenberg, L. (1990). Improving the accuracy of stereotypes in the workplace. Journal of management, 16(1), pp. 107-118.

(28) Bilides, D. (1990). Race, color, ethnicity and class: issues of biculturalism in school based adolescent counseling groups. Social work with groups, 13 (4), pp 43-58.

(29) Anthias, F., Yuval, D., Nira, C., & Cashmore, E. (1995). Racialized boundries: race, nation, gender, colour and class and the antiracist struggle. Book abstract.

(30) Wade, J. (1996). African American men's gender role conflict: The significance of racial identity. Sex Roles, 34(1-2), pp. 17-33.

(31) Cable, D. & Judge, T. (1996). Person-organization fit, job choice decisions and organizational entry. Organizational Behavior and Human Decision Processes, 67(3), 294-311.

(32) Allen, R. & Oshagan, H. (1995), An opportunity model: Some substantive and measurement concerns. National journal of sociology, 9(1), pp. 141-172.

(33) Hirschman, C. & Kraly, E. (1990). Racial and ethnic inequality in the United States, 1940 and 1950: the impact of geographic location and human capital. International Migration Review, vol 24, 1, p. 4-33.

(34) Hall, R. E. (1993). Clowns, buffoons, and gladiators: Media portrayals of African-American men. The Journal of Men's Studies,1, 239-251.

(35) Schmutte, P. & Ryff, C. (1997). Personality and well-being: Reexamining methods and meanings. Journal of Personality and Social Psychology, 73(3), 549-559.

(36) Biracial kids endure society's obsession with appearance. Los Angeles Sentinel (1995), July, 13, Sec A, p. 14, col 1.

(37) Grotevant, H. (1997). Family processes, identity development, and behavioral outcomes for adopted adolescents. Journal of Adolescent Research, 121), 139-161.

(38) Nobles, W. (1973). Psychological research and the black self concept: a critical review. Journal of Social Issues

(39) Cross, W. (1987). A two factor theory of black identity: implications for the study of identity development in minority children. Children's Ethnic Socialisation.

(40) Bowles, D. (1993). Bi-racial identity: Children born to African American and White couples. Clinical Social Work Journal, 21(4), 417-428.

(41) Hall, R. E. (1992). Bias among African-Americans regarding skin color: Implications for social work practice. Research on Social Work Practice, 2, 479-486.

(42) Jones, R. (1994). The end of Africanity? The Eurasian assault on Blackness. Western Journal on Black Studies, 18(4), 201-210.

(43) Martinez, E. (1993). Beyond Black/White: The racisms of our time. Social Justice, 20, 1-2(51-52), 22-34.

(44) McNeely, R. (1996). Review essay. Human relations, 49(4), pp. 489-499.

(45) Germain, C. (1991). Human Behavior in the Social Environment. Columbia University Press, New York, N.Y.

(46) Gatson, S. (July, 1994). Aristocrats of Color: The Black Elite, 1880-1920. Contemporary Sociology, 23(4), pp. 524-525.

X

Conclusion

The endowment of human beings with an acute sense of vision has proved potent in the organization of their social systems. Other means of perception merely serve to enhance the breadth and depth of humanity's visual senses. For lower species the ability of vision enables hunting and survival skills. For mankind, its use is much more complex, enabling the arrangement of values, norms, and other social phenomena into an organized hierarchy. Thus, vision, more than any other sense of perception, has allowed for the idealization of post-colonial criteria and stigmatization of anything society deems undesirable. Subsequently, in the aftermath of Western colonization light skin became the most desirable criteria of society and dark skin the most undesirable. Skin color served as vehicle of colonization and differentiation between the powerful and the powerless. Furthermore, light skin being endemic to the more powerful West evolved as the status ideal and basis of its social hierarchy between and among Asian-Americans and other people of color. Dark skin in contrast to light skin provided the means to extend colonization in which the continuation of domination could prevail by a less violent but equally effective course of action.

Of all the physical dimensions characteristic of the world's emerging diversity, light skin as American ideal has arguably the greatest social significance. Without vision, skin color cannot be perceived, but its implication remains constant in the absence of sight. Considering the biological function of skin, light skin has no fundamental dimension that dark skin does not have. Light skin has no innately distinct superiority that would set it apart from dark skin. Yet, those Asian-Americans who migrate to America and succeed do so based solely upon whether they are dark- or light-skinned. Subsequently it is the stigmatization of dark skin and the contrived notion of light skin superiority that has made the difference. For Asian-Americans who must assimilate into Western culture, this is critical to their life chances. If those who are stigmatized are not able to define and value who they are, they are likely to alter themselves as dictated by the imposition of Western ideals.

Beginning in the early 1800s, theories prevailed from Western literature that labeled people of color inferior. In this more modern post-colonial era the inferiority theory has been sanitized to suggest that such people are inferior due to their economic and social conditions or because they do not have the intellectual capacity to compete in an advanced technological society. Thus, in the minds of most citizens, whether the reason is biological or intellectual, dark skin characterizes people of color as inferior, conveniently negating any suggestions of racism, oppression, or otherwise colonization.

During the 1960s American intellectuals wrote about the pathology of people of color, and suggested special programs to better their situation. For decades the government funded special programs, which conservatives denounced as wasteful spending. Today they rationalize the pseudo-science of Herrenstein and Murray and others as evidence of the waste. The common assumption has been that if people of color fail to get admitted to college, obtain gainful employment, or locate housing then it must be the result of some personal inadequacy enhanced by liberal policies. Occasionally, when presented with an overwhelming amount of evidence, conservatives will concede that a racist landlord or a bigoted employer is to blame in exceptional cases. However, few will admit there are societal ideals built into the very fiber of Western civilization that are less obvious given the more overt manifestations of racism suggested in migration during recent history.

By definition, idealization of skin color like racism here refers to the efforts of a dominant group to exclude a dominated group from sharing in the material and symbolic rewards of status and power. It differs from the various other forms of exclusion in that qualification is contingent upon observable and assumed physiological traits. Such traits imply the inherent superiority of Euro-American groups, which are then rationalized as a natural order of the biological universe. The most zealous of the West profess that lighter-skinned Anglo-Saxon/Teutonic peoples are ideal, being superior to darker-skinned people as a matter of fact. In America they postulate that citizens of European descent have been uniquely endowed with the capacities necessary to bring about civilization. So-called "advancing civilization" was initially a thinly veiled form of color bias devoted to justifying aggression as the West embarked upon a worldwide mission aimed at conquering the darker-skinned masses. By way of colonization, the West left no domain of Asia and the remaining third world untouched. Their domination has necessitated a universal, almost mystic, idealization in the power of skin color, not race, to elevate or taint.

By exposition, the intolerant element of the power structure is the racial supremacist who for all intents and purposes has little to attach any sense of self-esteem other than their idealization of "whiteness." The supremacist is an exaggeration. To such a person Euro light skin is essential and can only be maintained through the domination of dark-skinned, color producing peoples. Additionally, because the myth of racial supremacy requires the concept of purity to function, assimilation is narrowly defined. The result is a heightened ability of those outside the group to threaten those within. Hence, the effort to assimilate Asian-Americans and other people of color has resulted in untold injustices and sufferings predicated upon Darwin's uncivilized notion of survival of the fittest. From that notion derives the experience of Asians who migrate West. It is, succinctly put, a manifestation of Darwin's survival confrontation between the stigmatized dark-skinned and the idealized Euro-light-skinned amid colonization.

The historical impact of colonization has predisposed migrant Asians in the post-millennium era to the internalization of ideals. In logic, their common experience with oppressed populations fostered a sense of commonality with similarly oppressed groups. However, under the circumstances Asian solidarity was disrupted. Among all people of color colonization remains a significant force in their oppression. Resultant oppression encouraged the application of Eurocentric ideals indiscriminately. The uppermost in status became those whose color approximates that of the mainstream. In an effort to circumvent humiliation, Asian-Americans accommodated a denigration of self. In the aftermath, their own oppression was enabled due to a differential in power. This differential motivated instances of stigmatization reflected in eurogamy and various other forms of hypergamy.

Much of the literature characterizes the institutionalization of Western ideals in a manner construed as beneficial to all light-skinned people. Nothing could be further from the truth. Light-skinned Asian-Americans were just as much a victim psychologically of the post-colonial hierarchy as the dark-skinned, albeit in a different manner. Unfortunately, dark-skinned Asians have always harbored a distrust of others based upon the idealization of light skin. No doubt, they have suffered greater stings of prejudice because their skin happens to be a potent contrast to the American ideal. But what all must realize is that light-skinned Asians are merely pawns in the process. To vent frustration on such members of the group encourages group demise. It may manifest as a host of social difficulties whose origins seem so elusive.

The idealization of light skin by Asian-Americans is a by-product of Western migration and attempts by outgroups to assimilate. Assimilation is not apart from the social problems among people of color in toto. All Asian-Americans want to succeed. From the brightest to the slowest of wit, regardless of skin color, all human beings desire success in life based upon valuing themselves and the goals they want to attain. When the legitimate avenues are cut off, people will resort to illegitimate and even harmful avenues.

When avenues are cut off completely, people will seek escape from reality. Those who do not experience this pessimism personally will be completely baffled trying to understand the self-destructive activities of others. To some extent all people of color who migrate West have had legitimate avenues to success cut off by the stigma associated with dark skin. To some extent they all have had to destroy a little of themselves to realize their goals. As a result, Asian-Americans are being denied success by the obstacles of a race/skin color power structure. More and more those who wear the label "third world" are encountering difficulties vis-à-vis post-colonization in their attempts at Western assimilation.

Some in the assimilated mainstream would probably be astonished to know that Asians and other people of color idealize one another on the basis of having light skin. The time and effort invested by them to do away with discrimination might somehow make them appear less given to practices that they have rallied against. But the idealization of light skin is a post-colonial issue that is deep rooted and complex. It is so institutionalized and, given America's world status, widely accepted that anyone who has migrated is affected by it. Those who settle in America to some extent give in to it once they arrive, regardless of their previous cultural experience.

As per Asian-Americans, the idealization of light skin has a long and established history. Contributing to ignorance is the fact that for decades "white" has been portrayed as the ultimate social phenomenon. It has become a psychosocial objective directed at people of color—particularly dark-skinned Asians. About the accuracy of this assumption, there should be no doubt. Notwithstanding, to then characterize oppression in a narrow "white" context does disservice to the scientific method. It enables the otherwise absurd rhetoric of hierarchy within a single species and in fact provides a conduit for the continued social, economic, and political domination of dark-skinned people. However deserving of sympathy, analyzing the role of victims is a necessity. Hence, never previously suggested, it is imperative to analyze the role played by

Asian-Americans and other victims in the stigmatization of people of color. While it is no doubt politically incorrect to cite victims or stray from the "white" perpetrator model, avoidance of it would be tantamount to fraud. The Asian-American role in the perpetuation of Western ideals is one of the fundamental dynamics of oppression in the post-colonial era.

A cursory review of the literature affirms a critical void in the analysis of skin color idealization. Not only are Euro Westerners consistently regarded as lone perpetrators but people of color are consistently regarded as victims—the black/white dichotomy. Eurogamy and the light-skinned among an increasingly indistinct population require that dialogue addressing so-called racism move from discussions of "race" to that of skin color. So-called racism is germane to the experience of dark-skinned people. As migrants, it makes Asians simultaneously victims and perpetrators. As victims, they remain second class citizens. As perpetrators, their behavior is a consequence of psychological colonization. It, thus, logically follows that population trends brought about by migration accommodate a view that America is no longer—or perhaps never was— a racially homogeneous civilization. It does not negate the pervasiveness of Western oppression but allows an amplified analysis to include the role played by all factions. Ultimately, it will benefit Asian-Americans by contributing to the knowledge base required for cooperation within a "multicultural" setting.

Asian-Americans as victims experienced immediate stigmatization once they emigrated to America. The Asian Exclusion Act of 1889, denied Asian emigrants the right to enter many Western territories. The assignment of Japanese citizens to "relocation centers" during WWII was unprecedented. Other similarly stigmatized people of color were denied the right to attend so-called public schools because they happened to serve "predominantly white" students during the 1880s. All three examples illustrate the involvement of Western governments and educational institutions in stigmatization by color for the perpetration of domination. Given the existence of stigmas at every level of Western civili-

zation, what prevails is then no longer a requirement vis-à-vis sustaining a sector of the ruling class. Colonization by stigma has
become so socially diffused that it is now an essential element of
the mediating process, through which much of the basic rewards
for the entirety of society are granted. In other words, the mechanisms for dominating Asian-Americans have become so complex
and intricate that they make it practically impossible to reverse
the process. The genesis of domination thus extends from the
American power structure that is arguably no longer relevant in a
multicultural world.

The stigmatization of dark skin in Western nations has also
had a devastating impact worldwide. Overtly motivated by the
racial supremacist and covertly condoned by the more tolerant
Western element, color is an unspoken factor in the various con-
frontations that dark-skinned males have had with Western institutions. Their color also correlates with a lack of economic and
political power, apparent in post-colonized nations where the West
has had considerable impact.

Through the 1970s America experienced economic difficulty.
That difficulty was rationalized as the result of social spending invested by "liberal" politicians who supported political efforts using
tax dollars to enhance quality of life for the less fortunate. This ush-
ered in the 1980s and a strong conservative backlash led by the then
leader of the Western world Ronald Reagan. Never uttered, but clearly
understood by all, was a need on the part of the power structure to
regain control of a government that appeared to have succumbed too
enthusiastically to the political pressures brought by people of color.
Such thinking is indicative of cultures dominated by males, where
the powerful ingroup is most threatened by outgroup males. The
psychological regard of the Western male for dark skin necessitates
that the dark-skinned Asian male poses the greatest threat, thus he
necessarily becomes the focus of control.

To its credit, America has begun to set standards, at least in
rhetoric to enable harmony among the various skin color factions.
Perhaps more than any other civilization, it encompasses a rich

mixture of hues, languages and religious philosophies. Unfortunately, what is to its credit has also caused problems. Increased
diversity has led to competition among the various groups for control of resources. Different languages and religions contribute to
the competition, but the color of skin is by far the focal point. In
an effort to control resources in their best interest, lighter-skinned
Euro groups have thus dominated the West to their benefit and
that of their skin color cohort, which includes an Asian-American
faction. Needless to say, the implications of skin color among Asian-
Americans are a microcosm of Western civilization. Where descendants of the colonial mainstream could have afforded to be indif-
ferent as pertains to color, migrant Asians as people of color least of
all cannot. Their nation of origin is effectively one of the masses of
poor, less powerful sovereignties subjected to the cultural inferiority suggested in dark skin. To enable assimilation and provide a
better life for themselves and their families, Asians—if they are to
remain viable—must join with others of color to redress characterization of dark skin in a more positive and self-conducive context.
Since their migration, this has been an all but impossible task.
The difficulty was facilitated by the power imbalance between the
two color opposites vis-à-vis the presence of color versus the absence of color. Efforts to confront the intolerant and support the
more tolerant among the mainstream to unite for a new raceless
world order would make for a considerable improvement.

Asian-Americans of all colors and creeds have some idea of
what colonization is and how it is manifested socially, politically,
and economically. They understand it is both covert and overt,
acted out by individuals and within the institutions they control.
That thought consistently congers up an image of dark-skinned
people suffering at the hands of their Western oppressors. As a
point of historical fact, such suffering cannot be denied. However,
current trends in eurogamy during an era of increased migration
necessitate a completely different strategy for conceptualizing oppression in the new millennium. Although "white" domination
will persist in essence, the West by virtue of increasing migration

must begin to conceptualize oppression in a less racial context. The objective of such a notion is an attempt to inform Asian-Americans in particular about the implications of skin color for their quality of life. The aim is to facilitate dialogue and enable the ability of the group and society to incorporate a new perspective that will accommodate recent shifts in the Western population. The specific focus is behavior that would otherwise be associated with colonialists. Unlike most of the literature to date, colonization here includes manifestations of stigmatization as they exist among Asians and other people of color. Hence, in Western terms the concept is frequently characterized as some malicious intentional overt act of individuals. In fact, as it occurs this is a half-truth. The more covert and seemingly harmless acts can be the most devastating. For example, a number of educators believe that community schools are the more efficient and practical way to run a school district; some university presidents regardless of race believe grade point averages (gpa) and "intelligence" tests should be the sole criteria for determining who gets into college. Such educators may not intend to stigmatize dark skin, but, when their beliefs result in the exclusion of certain segments of the population, then the belief qualifies as an act of colonization. Thus, contrary to the belief of many, the intention to stigmatize is not a precondition of colonization acts. In fact, unintended acts are similar to operating machinery that moves with unthinking, unfeeling deliberate speed. Much like a machine, those who take part in post-colonial oppression cannot be held accountable. Such impersonal objectivity is responsible for tolerating some of the most generic examples of hate crimes known in America. In order to comprehend, it will require an understanding that the dynamics of every major American institution operate on the basis that some degree of color stigmatization is acceptable. Whether it is rhetorically acceptable, it is at least expected and considered unavoidable. For example, the educational system accepts that dark-skinned students should have a markedly lower score on standardized tests. The norms of institutions are, in effect, standards for achievement.

They are the expectations that tell an individual what is required. When he/she starts challenging norms or aspiring beyond his/her designated role, he/she is punished or otherwise oppressed by the appropriate power structure. That power structure has produced volumes of literature pertaining to the stigmatization of dark skin, explaining the circumstances by which Asian-Americans and others are disserved.

Before migration, evidence was lacking that the various groups of color existed to stigmatize and/or colonize one another, although there was and continues to be competition. However, after having migrated West there is evidence among some of a change in attitude. The most potent problem in American post-colonization is the result that has perpetuated a status hierarchy among Asian-Americans based upon their proximity to Euro light skin. The emergence of euragamy increased their penchant for light skin and Eurasian children. Had this not occurred, inevitably a hierarchy might still exist. The prejudice and color variation, indicative of Western life in general, means that the variation within any group, given their identity strength, is susceptible to intragroup tension. In the midst of tension, light-skinned Asians are no less loyal to their ethnic roots, but are regarded somewhat differently by the West. This does not infer that life for them is bliss, but there is some advantage to having light skin in a culture where light skin is valued. Sometimes it may cause difficulty. It may reinforce hierarchies within both the mainstream and the "minority" community. The results push some to a marginal status that encourages additional problems based upon color. Thus, Asian-Americans of the various hues may guard feelings toward one another during social activities. Those in the community of whatever color play a role in this hierarchy, but the lighter-skinned are stigmatized less in Western society because they are endowed with attributes that compliment it. As a result, light-skinned Asian-Americans may make their way with relative ease in the circles even of the most conservative mainstream while the same ability for their darker-skinned counterparts is all but impossible regardless of background.

Considering the extent of colonization, to suggest special programs to alleviate it is moot. It is true that conditions are pathological for a disproportionate number of those characterized by dark skin, but the situation will not improve by funding ineffective programs. Asian-Americans are obviously not inferior as would be implied by "special" programs. Thus, it is plausible that much of the problem extends from the fact that the larger American society forces dark-skinned people to live under inferior conditions. The larger society has also decided that there is no need to build low-rent housing; it has chosen instead to invest in "white" communities, to provide minority communities with inadequate education and social services, and to man the area with an oppressive, violent police force, whose function is to keep them subjugated. In other words, much of the inferior, pseudo-science associated with dark skin is the direct result of colonial rhetoric.

In the design and utilization of social programs, the extent of colonization is either ignored or America is in fear of acting to eliminate it for political and social reasons. As program after program fails, blame is assigned to victims who are least able to effectively advocate on their own behalf, as in the case of Vincent Chin. Popular rationales are offered, such as "they did not follow through," "the program was out of touch," "the funding was insufficient," and so on. Every solution is suggested except the all out abolition of the color issue from society entirely. Its ability to threaten the status quo keeps it secure and intact. Otherwise eliminating Euro ideals will require much more than dealing with acts by individuals against individuals or particular groups against other groups.

Unfortunately, the root causes of American problems and their crippling effects continue to be a factor in the most basic institutions of daily life. Such institutions—education, housing, public law, etc.—have forced Asian-Americans to the fringes of society on the notion that their color denotes them as inferior. Overt segregation in earlier decades was assured by color given America's greater homogeneity and less miscegenation. There is no one cure-all for skin color and other post-colonial issues among Asian-Americans.

Problems with skin color cannot be alleviated by governmental programs funded by tax dollars. What will eventually alleviate it begins with the acknowledgement of its existence. That acknowledgement must come from both the dominant light-skinned and dominated darker-skinned populations. Furthermore, on the part of Asian-Americans, both light- and dark-skinned, a will must manifest to value self and identity internally as opposed to externally via Western ideals for light skin. Above all, a movement must eventually come about that will redefine the implications of dark skin, not only in America, but in an increasingly diverse global community as well!

INDEX

Abyssinia, 43

Afrasians, 112-13

Africa: Afrikaners in, 29; and blood heritage, 202; Christianity in, 21-24, 26-27; color in, 13-16, 24-25, 29; first encounters in, 14, 21-22; human origins in, 12-13, 16; and pygmies, 161. *See also* Abyssinia; Egypt; Ethiopia; skin color; South Africa

African American: civil rights, 68; dating patterns, 41; racism, 62, 63, 64

Afro-Nicaraguans, 38-39

Agatharchides, 14

Akkadians, 43

Allport, Gordon, 14, 177

Amanda (case study), 107-109

American Association for Ethiopian Jews, 44

Americans: as immigrants, 39-40, 55-56; Hispanic, 94-95

Antebellum South, rhetoric of the, 18, 26-27, 62

Arabs, 43

Asclepiades, 16

Ashcroft, L., 124

Asia, skin color in, 153,154

"Asian", 86-92, 98-99

Asian-American(s): assimilation of, 54-58, 64, 69, 74, 81, 87-91, 102-107, 111-20, 217-19; bias, 81-82; and Bleaching Syndrome, 114-15; and crime, 182, 184-87; and dark skin, 57, 58, 102, 125; denied success, 180, 218; and education, 104-105, 173-75, 178-79; and exogamy, 59, 107; expression, 175; gangs, 183-86; groups in the U.S., 180-81; and light skin, 40, 58, 115, 125-26, 218; and light skin ideals, 103, 105, 107, 214-15, 218, 223; migration patterns, 55-56, 111; as minorities, 64, 102, 104, 125-26, 136; murder of, 70-73, 181, 182; and political naïveté of, 63-64, 75; and power, 218; and racism, 54, 57-75; refugee waves, 180-81; and self, 209, 217; and sexuality,

guilt, 128-29; and health risks, 125-28, 132-42; and Hispanic bias, 82-85; historically beautiful, 15-16; ideals, 98, 154; importance of, 57, 59; and India, 16; and Israel, 44; and Japan, 65, 66; and Jews, 44- 45, 46-48; low value of, 89-90, 196-97; and Native Americans, 16; and racial profiling, 130, 131; and racism, 137, 220; and Semites, 43-48; stereotypes, 216-17; stigma, 218, 220, 222, 223. *See also* endogamy; eurogamy; exogamy; stereotypes

Darwin, Charles, 12, 216. *See also* evolution; natural order

Davidson, Rachel, 41

Davis, L., 185

Debt, The (Bogle), 192-93

democratic process, 124, 142, 143, 175

denigration, 22, 36-38, 46, 47; Asian-American, 58, 73, 104, 114, 124; mechanisms, 17, 27, 28, 31, 68-69

Denver, Colorado, 29, 197

Detroit, Michigan, 70-72

discrimination: childhood, 14-15; dark skin, 44; genesis of, 17; and global skin color bias, 42-43; reverse, 197, 198

"domination model", 87

"Double Consciousness", 35, 36. *See also* "passing"

Draper, Robert, 107

"Dual Perspective", 37

DuBois, W. E. B., 35, 36

Ebens, Ronald, 70-72

education: and Asian-Americans, 104-105, 173-75, 178-79; and stigma, 223

effort versus ability, 174

Egypt, 15

Ehrlich, Howard, 177

employment and discrimination, 193, 199, 204

empowerment, 123, 125. *See also* power

gangs, 183-86
Garifuna, 39
gender: and eurogamy, 105-106; and racism, 67-68
"generalized other", 36-37
genotype, 13, 42, 86, 88, 105, 112, 117, 136, 172
Gentleman's Quarterly (magazine), 107
Germany, 55, 56, 162, 176; light-skin in, 15
grassroots movement, 123
Great Britain, 14, 55-56, 155; colonization by, 38, 89, 102;
endogamy in, 87; social science in, 176
Greek norms of beauty, 14, 15, 16-17, 20
group membership, 39, 40, 41, 86, 207
Guam, 126
guilt, 26

hair, 13, 16, 108, 116, 153, 160, 161, 166, 197
Hall, Ronald E., 40, 104, 137, 195
Ham and Africa, 24-25, 26-27
Hawaii, 110, 165
health: and cancer, 137, 139-40, 141; and hypertension, 127, 132-37; and media, 140-42
Hector and Gamble, 116-17
hegemony, 48, 102, 184, 202, 206
Herodotus, 16
Herrenstein, 215
Hicks, Joe, 65
hierarchy: and Asian-American skin color, 66-67, 70, 75, 92; mechanisms, 68-69, 104, 214; and skin color, 10, 45, 66, 66, 69, 102, 110, 217, 218, 223
Hispanic-Americans, 40; and bias, 82-84, 88, 94-98, 111; and light skin, 83, 84, 85, 86, 98
Hispanic(s), 110, 111, 155-56; colonization, 82-86, 87
Hmong, 179, 180
Hoetink, Harry, 16, 73

205; and exogamy, 91, 105; in Germany, 15; and Hispanics,83, 84, 85, 86, 98; ideals, 87, 89-91, 98, 154-55; in Israel, 47-48; and Japan, 58, 59, 87; preferences, 39-40; and prosperity, 199, 201, 203; and self, 40; stereotypes, 217. *See also* endogamy; eurogamy; exogamy; "passing"; power

Lin, Mee Ying, 63

Lippmann, 177

Livingstone, David, 14

Loeb, R., 81

"looking glass self " (Cooley), 207

Los Angeles, California, 58, 64, 65, 85

lynching, 27, 194, 199, 200

Ma, Ying, 60-65, 71, 73

"mail order bride", 107-10, 155

Malaysians, 110

marriage: criteria, 103, 105, 114, 156; endogamy, 103; exogamy, 103; eye shape and, 103, 105; Hmong, 179; and intermarriage, 85, 86, 112; interracial, 91, 92; "mail order", 107, 155; and skin color bias, 89-90, 153. *See also* "Passing"

marry in. *See* endogamy

marrying "white", 107

marry out. *See* exogamy

Marsh, 14, 15

"master status", 47, 57, 200-201

McIntosh, P., 74

Mead, G., 36, 207

media: advertising, 119; film, 117-18, 192-94; and health, 140-42; and identity, 193, 192-95, 198; and integration, 194; magazine, 119, 155; power, 130; print, 128-29, 131, 141, 194-95; and stereotypes, 128-29; television, 111, 129

medium skin, 93-94, 96, 98

melanin, 18, 132
Mestizos, 39, 59, 152-53
metaphors, 19, 26, 30
Mettger, W., 141
Mexican-Americans, 40, 85
Michigan, 70-73, 159, 164, 169, 170
Michigan State University, 157
migration: and Asian bias, 81-82; patterns, 55-56, 111
"minorities", 88; Asian-Americans as, 64, 102, 104,
          125-26, 136
Miskitos, 39
missionaries, 21-24
"model minority", 172-73, 175, 177, 178-79, 180-81,
          183, 185-86
Mongoloids, 13, 19, 86. *See also* Asian-Americans mulatto
          ("tragic mulatto"), 192-94, 196, 199, 202, 203, 205
"mulatto hypothesis", 196 murder, 29, 70-7, 75, 181, 182,
          184; and eurogamy, 108-109, 129
Murray, 61
Murray, 215

NAACP, 195
Nagata, D., 175
National Taiwan University, 67
Native Americans, 16-17, 29, 116, 157, 198
natural order, 36, 37, 216, 217-18; and evolution, 12, 42,
          172. *See also* Darwin
Neal, A. M., 40
Negritos, 161, 162, 164
Negroids, 13, 19
Negros, Philippines, 160, 161
Netherlands, 55
New Jersey, 130-31, 137
New York, 131, 137
New York City, New York, 62, 105, 128, 194

of, 82, 89; and skin color, 18, 43, 214, 216, 218, 220, 223

projection, 19, 20-21, 26-28

Puerto Rico, and light skin, 40, 94-95

pygmies, 161

race: awareness of, 14; defined, 13; rhetoric, 19

Race Relations (Kitano), 87

racial profiling, 130, 131

racial supremacy, 35, 216, 221-22

racial values, 114, 115

racism: African-American, 62, 63, 64; American, 18, 29, 73-75; Asian, 55, 57-75; and "black racism", 61-65; and "brown racism", 59; Chinese, 59, 61-63; as a dark skin phenomenon, 137, 220; defined, 36, 56, 191, 216; and epithets, 60-62, 66, 70, 111; and gender, 67-68; global, 36-50, 74-75; global model of, 55; and ideals, 215, 217, 224-25; and identity, 191; institutionalized, 73, 138; in Japan, 58-59, 65; in Korea, 65; and migration, 55-56; and "model minority", 172-73, 175, 177, 178-79, 180-81, 183, 185-86; and oppression, 222; as skin color, 127-31, 219; skin-color enabled, 37, 41, 58, 74, 90, 102, 219, 243; and skin color hierarchy, 40, 43-44, 45; and stereotypes, 61, 128-29, 185; U.S., 59, 60-69; and violence, 29, 71, 182-85; "white", 59, 75; Ying Ma's view of, 60-61. *See also* caste; Chin; language; Ma; power; women

rape, 27, 109, 129, 184

Rape of Nanking (Chang), 66

reaction-formation, 20

Reagan, Ronald, 220

"red", 19

relocation centers, 219

Republic of China, 60, 66, 67

research, 67, 73, 83, 91; medical, 127, 134-35, 138; social

science, 172, 174, 177, 192
Russell, K., 137

Salter, P., 178
San Antonio, Texas, 85
San Francisco, California, 63, 64
Sciara, F. J., 40
segregation, 27
self concept, 36-37; and dark skin, 85; of Ethiopian Semites, 47-48; and light skin, 40; and racism, 68; and self hate, 86
Semites, 43-48. *See also* Ethiopia; Israel
sexuality, 21, 26-28, 173-74. *See also* rape
"significant other", 36, 37
Simon, R., 124
Sinha, A., 67
skin color: in Asia, 153,154; bias, 42, 81-86, 99; and black/white dichotomy, 191, 192, 204, 209; and colonization, 30-31, 214; compensation, 47; dictates environment, 30; dominance, 48; and existential reality, 49, 172, 173; and fear, 14; function, 37-39, 214; global domination and, 41, 42; global preferences and, 36-49; and health, 127, 132, 137, 139-40, 141; hierarchy, 10, 45, 66, 66, 69, 102, 110, 217, 218, 223; ideals, 91-98, 154-68, 200, 214-19; in Japan, 58, 59, 65, 66, 87; Jewish, 45; and latitude, 25; and melanin, 18, 132; and metaphors, 19, 26, 30; and "minority", 88; mythos, 19-20, 24-25; negative views of, 18-30; norms, 15, 16; origins, 12-13, 25; and power, 18, 43, 214, 216, 218, 220, 223; psychology of, 17, 18-19, 26; and racism, 127-31, 219; and rejection, 38-40; and sexuality, 21, 26-28, 173-74; and social aspects, 30-31; and status, 39, 47-48; and taboo, 9-10, 28, 84, 118; terms, 19; as a threat, 125, 127, 128. *See also*

Printed in the United States
778300001B